D1722996

Esther Reginbogin

Buster Keaton and Modern European Drama

An American Filmmaker Anticipating Aesthetic Multiplicity

Diplomica Verlag

Reginbogin, Esther: Buster Keaton and Modern European Drama. An American Filmmaker Anticipating Aesthetic Multiplicity, Hamburg, Diplomica Verlag 2022

Buch-ISBN: 978-3-96146-932-1
PDF-eBook-ISBN: 978-3-96146-432-6
Druck/Herstellung: Diplomica Verlag, Hamburg, 2022

Bibliografische Information der Deutschen Nationalbibliothek:
Die Deutsche Nationalbibliothek verzeichnet diese Publikation in der Deutschen Nationalbibliografie; detaillierte bibliografische Daten sind im Internet über http://dnb.d-nb.de abrufbar.

© Diplomica Verlag, Imprint der Bedey & Thoms Media GmbH
Hermannstal 119k, 22119 Hamburg
http://www.diplomica-verlag.de, Hamburg 2022
Printed in Germany

The unexpected was our staple product, the unusual our object, and the unique was the ideal we were always hoping to achieve.

Buster Keaton

Table of Contents

Buster Keaton and his silent film comedies in the light of aesthetic developments in modern European drama

> Pure visual comedy has been dead [...] in cinema, although people often talk about it as if it were still there. [...] Visual comedy [is] closer to dreams than to humor [...] Keaton [...] made a few perfect visual movies, whose corny themes became actual filmed myths. He realised, from shot to shot, dreamlike entities from the American and universal subconscious [...].[1]

Buster Keaton originally came from the theatre as he was practically born and raised on the American vaudeville stage.[2] From there, he transferred ideas and techniques to the art form he became most famous for: silent film comedy. Around the same time Keaton began to establish himself as a highly inventive filmmaker, a new form of European theatre was emerging. In breaking away from the naturalism and rationalism that had been dominating its stages, twentieth-century European dramatists completely revolutionized the nature and meaning of theatrical representation. They did so first and foremost through concepts of dramatic writing and performance that had never been seen before.

The aim of this study is to discover certain comic ideas as well as concrete techniques in Keaton's art of performance and filmmaking that anticipated the multiple aesthetic concepts developped by European dramatists in the twentieth century. At first sight, it does not seem exactly appropriate to compare silent film comedy, an art form basically relying on farce and vaudeville, with a form of drama where non-communication gains increasingly in communicative power, where the serious and the grotesque are no longer separable, and where reality forces playwrights to make social, political and ontological statements. This is why the similarities between Buster Keaton's art and modern European theatre analyzed here might, in many cases, rather be called affinities.

On the one hand, it is certainly true that Keaton came into film by pure accident. Accordingly, he instinctively drew on vaudeville with its main emphasis on physical dexterity. Yet, he did not approach film as if it were filmed theatre. On the contrary: although he never established a written theory, his comedies convey aesthetic ideas behind gags, camera angles and other, highly sophisticated techniques that are evidence not only of his extremely being conscious of the possibilities the new medium offered, but also of his intending more than comic simplicity that makes people laugh. While categorizing his art or putting labels such as distanciation, alienation, tragicomedy, or absurd on his achievements would not do justice to Keaton, it could be argued that he did pave the way for the kind of artistic freedom that came to flourish on twentieth-century European stages. His approach to mise-en-scène can even be seen as a prerequisite for the ideological and dramatic freedom that was to completely transform the nature of theatre.

It is especially interesting to analyze techniques which, while still creating a comic effect in Keaton's films, increasingly became tools in modern European drama to convey the serious, frequently tragicomic, and even tragic condition of modern man. A comparison of those techniques, therefore, is best based on the confrontation of contrasts even though, of course, it is not always possible to directly relate film to theatre. At this point, it should be mentioned that, as to Buster Keaton, this study will be focussing exclusively on the era between 1920 and 1928 when he created his masterpieces in silent film comedy (even though he did not direct all the films he starred in). Equally important, all European dramatists discussed here were influenced by or even worked themselves in cinema.[3]

Assessing how Keaton's conscious use of the medium film anticipates the use of meta-theatrical devices by twentieth-century European dramatists best starts with looking at Bertolt Brecht and Luigi Pirandello and their respective techniques of *Verfremdung* and *aesthetic distance.* Both playwrights put their emphasis on the act of narrating and presenting as well as on the act of watching. Just as the actor's self-consciousness reveals itself in their dealing with their own condition both in relation to their art and the character they portray, the spectator becomes aware of their own explicit position as observer. The critical and meta-theatrical comment typical of early twentieth-century European plays increasingly turns into an expression of social, political and ontological concerns in plays written in the second half of the century. In these works, the above-mentioned distance leads to the *Entfremdung* from the self, which is occasionally already present in Keaton's films as well as demonstrated in words and mise-en-scène in Brecht's works, but even more so in Eugène Ionesco's plays.[4] The human being even loses their human nature in their attempt to comply with the surrounding world which, for its part, becomes more and more irrational itself. The dramatic situation turns grotesque when the animate and inanimate world force the human body to transform itself in order to be able to survive. Whereas Keaton expresses these modern concerns while still remaining true to farce and vaudeville devices, in modern European theatre, a new dramatic language emerges. First initiated by Alfred Jarry and Antonin Artaud, it is further developped by the playwrights of the Theatre of the Absurd, and especially by Ionesco and Samuel Beckett who put the form of theatrical representation as well as existence itself into question.

This analysis is intended to demonstrate Buster Keaton's position between theatre and film, old and new techniques, simple and sophisticated devices, dream and reality. He could express these antagonisms only in film as '[…] the greatest thing to me about picture making was the way it automatically did away with the physical limitations of the theatre'[5].

I. Using the medium to expose the art of performance

The fact that Buster Keaton originally came from the stage appears to have made him especially aware of the respective possibilities film and theatre offer for pointing out the differences between the two. It seems like a paradox, then, that Keaton made use of techniques which – cinematically – resembled those Bertolt Brecht and Luigi Pirandello would lay down in aesthetic concepts and put into practice in their plays. He thereby came close to and virtually anticipated Brecht's *Verfremdungseffekt* and Pirandello's theory of *aesthetic distance*. It is important to bear in mind, though, that Keaton created films that were first and foremost comic without their forgoing an occasional serious note.

1. Presentation aiming at surprise and laughter

Buster Keaton never grew tired of pointing out that his primary intention was to make people laugh. He preferred the comic effect to the logical narrative line. It is not the story and its outcome that shall capture the audience's attention (although they normally do). With him, these elements are subordinate to surprises and gags, even more so than in Charlie Chaplin's films. In his book *The Theater and Cinema of Buster Keaton*, Robert Knopf clearly distinguishes between gags and stunts that disrupt the narrative line and those that serve it. He argues that many of the physical acts Keaton performs in his films are a reminder both of the *lazzi* – independent interludes between scenes in the Italian *commedia dell'arte* – and of the vaudeville tradition. Knopf goes on to explain that Keaton's gags are mostly adapted to and thus integrated into the art of filmmaking itself.[6] For the purpose of this chapter, the comic moments that arise without any necessary contextual relationship are, therefore, the more interesting ones to look at.

1.1. 'Verfremdung', 'aesthetic distance' and tragicomic opposition

In her book *Contemporary Italian Filmmaking: Strategies of Subversion – Pirandello, Fellini, Scola, and the Directors of the New Generation*, Manuela Gieri compares in detail the concepts of Brecht's *Verfremdung* (which she translates as 'estrangement') and of Pirandello's *aesthetic distance*. She argues that Brecht, despite his demand to present the familiar as unfamiliar, strives to achieve a re-composition of narrative and epic and thus to establish a historical continuity that also informs his notion of man as being conditioned by history and milieu. Brecht's spectator naturally passes a critical comment on the events enacted before their eyes as the meta-theatrical nature of acting and presenting prevents the audience from submitting to a cathartic experience, instead arousing curiosity in the very act of representation itself. Pirandello, on the other hand, regards 'humoristic dissociation' as essential for structuring the entire process of mise-en-scène. His characters never succeed in reconciling their being and appearing. The spectator's critical attitude and with it their distance from what they witness onstage result from this tragicomic opposition.[7]

Drawing a fine distinction between humour and the comic, Pirandello explains in his essay *L'Umorismo*[8] (1908) that the comic effect arises from contradictions: 'Il comico è appunto un *avvertimento del contrario*.'[9] It is, therefore, always reflection, that is an active thought process, about the origins of and reasons for the contradiction presented that leads '[...] oltre a quel primo avvertimento, o piuttosto, più addentro: da quel primo *avvertimento del contrario* mi ha fatto passare a questo *sentimento del contrario*'[10]. This reflection must be visible in the work of art in order to be effective as it '[...] lo analizza, spassionandosene; ne scompone l'imagine'[11]. Only reflection and analysis provoke the spectator's detachment from the plot and its characters and thus the *aesthetic distance* necessary for arousing laughter.

The different ways Keaton chooses to record and present things, people and events create an effect that often can be described as similar to the one pursued and achieved by Bertolt Brecht in his plays a few years later. On some occasions, Keaton lets images appear as bizarre and other than 'normal'. The most illustrative example is the sequence in *The Cameraman* (1928) where the main character, Luke Shannon, played by Keaton, presents his first 'film' to the news agency he wants to work for. Not even complete in their recording, the images are dissolving into each other rather than following one another, thus overlapping on the screen: an ocean liner seems to be floating on an avenue right towards the audience in the agency's projection room, while cars appear to be running through the people on the street. So instead of showing 'reality' captured on film, Shannon/Keaton offers an artefact of wildly amalgamated pieces that has a surrealistic touch. It is this contradiction between 'true' reality and filmed reality made visible by meta-artistic means that makes us, the spectators, aware of the process of presentation. The effect resembles Bertolt Brecht's *Verfremdungseffekt*, meaning that '[...] vieles, was natürlich schien, sollte als künstlich erkannt werden'[12]. Although this is an extreme and rare example, it shows Keaton's awareness that film, more so than theatre, enables the artist to play with reality by presenting his character's own – artificial – version of an 'objective' reality.

There is also a sense of 'humoristic dissociation' present in this scene as both Shannon and the film he has made are not what they appear to be. The entire staff of the agency laughs at the 'capacities' of Luke Shannon as a cameraman and his weird assembly of images. As to us, the audience of *The Cameraman* itself, it is by the recognition of the very contrast between being and appearing as manifest here in the character of Shannon that we perceive the serious, if not the tragic, as coexisting alongside the comic impression.

It is clear that Buster Keaton does not go as far as to prevent the spectator from feeling sympathy for Keaton's character and his failed attempt to impress the agency's owners. Nonetheless, the nature of this disastrous film projection, while tragic for the character, appears comic to the audience. Again, it is this sense of tragicomic opposition that provokes the spectator's laughter at the character and the situation he finds himself in. At the same time, this contrast arouses a feeling of surprise among the audience at the result of Shannon's work. In this respect, Keaton creates an effect similar to the one analyzed by Pirandello in his theory of *aesthetic distance*.

1.2. The frame as a means to create a tragicomic effect

The surprise effect is also achieved through the opposition of stillness and motion. In Keaton's films, this contrast is most powerfully represented in the visual relationship between the frame on the one hand and the action happening within and outside this frame on the other. The camera becomes a highly manipulative tool.

The presence of the frame is best underlined when the camera is being used as an active element to fix or widen the filmic space. At the beginning and the end of *The Cameraman*, Keaton's character, Luke Shannon, is shown standing alone with his camera in an empty space. The frame does not shift. In the first scene, a crowd of cheering people and reporters with their cameras suddenly invade the space around him. Instantly, Keaton finds himself in the middle of chaos. As soon as all this has started, it is over. The square, filling the entire screen, is empty again, except for Shannon now being in the company of Sally, the girl working at the news agency he is seeking a job with as a reporter. These two figures are now the active centre of the deserted square. Likewise, at the end of the film, Shannon is alone again, standing in front of the news agency when Sally comes running into the frame to tell him that he has just been hired as a professional photographer. In both sequences, the camera, and thus the frame, remains immobile.

The surprise element arises as motion from outside the frame disrupts the stillness inside the frame. In the film's opening sequence, in particular, the experience for the character is rather serious. The sudden invasion not only destroys the feeling of peace and certainty, but, more importantly, proves that the main character does not fit into society or at least not into the circles he aspires to belong to. The image of the rejected and isolated figure that is confronted with the cheering crowd makes the character's situation appear both comic and tragic. It is the awareness of this opposition between the comic and the tragic which makes the audience laugh while still arousing sympathy for Shannon.

A tragicomic effect is equally created through the camera's moving and enlarging the frame. At the end of *The Cameraman*, Shannon, filming a regatta, witnesses Sally going overboard when the boat she has been sitting in with her admirer, Stagg, makes a sharp turn. Shannon immediately leaves his recording device to save the girl from drowning while her companion seeks safety on the beach. In this sequence, two cameras are at work: the real film camera and Shannon's camera. After Shannon has left his position at the camera, it is the real film camera's moving backwards which reveals that Shannon's camera continues to be operated by his little monkey. (When this film is projected later at the agency, the spectator becomes aware of Keaton's highly sophisticated use of the medium film: some shots filmed by the monkey are clearly identical with those recorded by the real film camera, while other shots make it obvious through different camera angles that the events were recorded by two cameras.) It is exactly when the frame widens and the monkey is shown being busy at Shannon's camera that the true surprise occurs. At this moment, Shannon is seen in complete stillness, sunken to his knees at discovering that Sally is walking off with Stagg, her 'rescuer'. This shot arouses pity in the spectator for the tragic figure whose loneliness and motionless posture set him in sharp contrast to the wide space and the waves of the ocean behind him. Yet, the fact that it is the monkey who captures Shannon's disbelief on film makes an equally moving and amusing impression on the spectator. This discovery does not allow the audience to merely indulge in sympathy for the character. More importantly, it makes them consciously register the surprise effect that is created through the moving frame.

All the devices that have been discussed so far do not have an exact equivalent in theatre as they are of a purely film-technical nature. What is of importance here is that they cause surprise by revealing the coexistence of the comic and the tragic within characters, situations and events. This surprise effect creates a certain distance between the spectator and the action unfolding onscreen, preventing the spectator from being entirely mesmerized by what they are seeing.

2. Exposing the process of artistic creation

Unveiling the process of both creating and experiencing art was one if not *the* basic concern of nearly every artistic field in the first half of the twentieth century, and especially of European drama. Likewise, the film screen became medium and space to expose performance as performance, thus altering the relationship between the artist and their work of art as well as that between the spectator and the representation they witness. To make the audience aware of how a story is being told, Keaton and modern European dramatists often chose to play with the traditional linear plot, yet each of them to a different extent. Keaton particularly drew attention to the devices that, in com- bination with his skills as a performer, created the comic. It is not so much the happy ending but the way the comic disrupts or serves a story that is emphasized in his films.

2.1. Discontinuity through the multiplicity of narratives and their presentation

As Walter Benjamin explains in *Versuche über Brecht*, European theatre in the twentieth century evolved into 'episches Theater', epic theatre, with the stage becoming a so-called 'Ausstellungsraum', that is an exhibition space where the act of representation is literally made visible and every spectator is an observer with their own special interests.[13] Buster Keaton, of course, never chose such a radical approach. At times, though, he does allow the audience to focus on the act of story-telling rather than the story itself. He achieves this effect primarily by interspersing the plot with gags and twists that are more essential for the story than logical smoothness.

One device to underline the act of telling a story consists in presenting it in various versions. In *The Three Ages* (1923), Buster Keaton's first feature-length comedy and a parody of D.W. Griffith's *Intolerance*[14], the same story is told three times (with the same actors). The first version takes place in the Stone Age, the second one in the Roman Age, and the third one in the 1920s. Every plot is divided into sequences, with each sequence being presented separately in the respective period of time. By choosing this method of representation, Keaton draws the spectator's attention away from the storyline. As Robert Knopf observes, '[s]ince the story and outcome remain essentially the same in each era, the focus shifts from *what* will happen to *how* it will happen, emphasizing the variety of ways Keaton performs similar gags from era to era'[15]. The spectator is invited to consciously watch the artist's techniques of storytelling just as the artist consciously uses them. Through their respective awareness of the act of representation, both the artist and the spectator gain their own distance in relation to the story.

With regard to Keaton, this awareness is essentially vital as his art originated from impro-visation. An idea, a prop, or even just a gag were enough to spark off an entire comedy. This technique stemmed from the vaudeville tradition where the audience followed the action onstage without being led to focus on how it was being presented. In *The Three Ages*, by contrast, it is precisely Keaton's meta-artistic approach to presenting the plot that defines and emphasizes the variation of his comic ideas – and vice versa.

By playing with exclusively filmic devices, Keaton equally makes the spectator recognize the possibilities for destroying the illusory character of film itself that are inherent in the art of film-making. Long before the camera became the centre of action and attention in *The Cameraman*, he had already used it as an explicit tool in some of his early films. In those works, he considered and treated the camera not only as a recording device but also as a technical instrument that enabled him to establish a relationship between himself – the artist – and the audience. Walter Kerr claims that it was Keaton who '[…] called attention to the camera's presence as a barrier'[16], thus making the spectator become aware of their position. The camera is there, the artist is free to play with it.

Although Keaton prefers long shots in order to create a distinctive effect (a phenomenon discussed later in this study), there are moments in his films when the camera – and with it the spectator – is literally at the character's heels. In these instances, the comic hero and the spectator share the same experience, most often that of surprise. The entire chase sequence in *Cops* (1922) is built on this principle. Each time the main character, Buster, has managed to delude the policemen and is shown in an empty space, the perspective changes, with the house walls on either side of the street forming the natural frame of the image. Only after a fraction of time does the entire apparatus of men come running around the corner and thus into view for Buster as well as the spectator. With the action initially being hidden from the protagonist's and the spectator's eyes, they both experience a feeling of surprise. Yet, its effect on them is entirely different. While the hero realizes that for him the consequences are serious, the spectator's reaction is laughter. This prevents the audience from identifying with the character's situation and the filmic reality at large.

Another scene where the presence of the camera – and the power in the hands of the artist to play with it – is highlighted occurs in the short film *One Week* (1920). While the wife of Keaton's character is taking a bath, the soap falls onto the floor. In order to allow her to reach it and to remain undisturbed by the audience's view in this delicate moment, a hand covers the lens. Preventing the spectator from watching the action that still continues makes them aware of their position as observer. It is a silent comment that, precisely by interrupting the process of watching without halting the actual continuity of the action, provokes the spectator's detachment from the events unfolding onscreen.

In disrupting the continuity of the story line by relying on purely cinematic devices, Keaton achieves an effect comparable to the *Verfremdungseffekt* as advocated by Bertolt Brecht. In this context, though, it is important to understand how the comic in the works of both artists is defined through their respective use of meta-artistic means. Keaton employs meta-filmic devices to literally stage his vaudeville stunts. Through this kind of mise-en-scène, he creates the basically comic nature of his silent films without dismissing the occasionally serious note. Brecht, for his part, draws on meta-theatrical devices to underline his plays' often sarcastic criticism of contemporary political and social circumstances, allowing only for an underlying – mostly bitter – comic.[17]

2.2. Discontinuity through the fusion of reality, art and illusion

Exposing performance as performance, thus, constitutes the main approach to putting the process of presentation and representation into the foreground. The meta-theatrical mise-en-scène has two objectives: to clarify the actor's relation to the act of representation as well as to determine the spectator's position during the act of watching imaginary events. It could be argued that also silent film, by its very nature, prevents the spectator from taking illusion for reality as the disruption of visual continuity through inserting intertitles and the lack of spoken language affect the process of identification. Interestingly, though, Buster Keaton uses intertitles rather sparingly in his films, relying more on visual than verbal clarification; often, they serve a comic aim instead of an explanatory one.

At the beginning of the twentieth century, the idea of crossing the boundary separating art and reality became highly attractive to both theatre and film artists. One similarity between some of Keaton's films and Pirandello's plays, especially, lies in the multiplicity of layers characterizing the respective structures of these works. The different layers comprise reality and illusion but also different kinds of illusion. While Keaton frequently presents the plot within the plot in the form of a dream, Pirandello does so in the form of a theatrical event.

In modern European theatre, crossing the boundary between illusion and reality increasingly meant breaking down the fourth wall. Film, of course, can only allude to or play with this concept. Buster Keaton offers a perfect example in his third feature film, *Sherlock Jr.* (1924), when, in a dream sequence, his main character literally steps into and out of a film screen. *Sherlock Jr.* consists of two stories – a frame story and a dream which, in turn, becomes itself a film – where the 'real' characters are also the main characters in the protagonist's dream. It is obvious that only the protagonist himself, a projectionist in a film theatre, can be the hero in this dreamed world. By fusing characters and paralleling plots – as naturally happens in dreams –, Keaton blurs the lines between illusion of art, illusion of dream and reality of life, thus exposing film as being just as illusory as dreams. In *The Playhouse* (1921), Keaton combines dream and theatre in a double twist as, in his dream, he himself is the theatre event, being everyone from actors to spectators and musicians.

Around the same time in Europe, Luigi Pirandello made an aesthetic out of using the meta-artistic principle to show art as art in plays such as *Sei Personaggi in Cerca d'Autore* (1921)[18] and *Ciascuno a suo Modo* (1925)[19]. Like *Sherlock Jr.* and *The Playhouse*, both of Pirandello's plays are built on two different layers. In *Ciascuno a suo Modo*, the play's 'reality' constitutes the frame story whose characters are the 'audience' of a play within the play, that is the second layer. Some members of this 'audience' then become the 'characters' of the play within the play who stage their own lives. Through this double-layered approach, the act of someone presenting something or representing someone is underlined. Again, the aim here is to establish a distance between the audience and the story: what the spectator is watching is something that is being enacted.

It was Bertolt Brecht who formulated the demand 'Das Zeigen muss gezeigt werden' in a poem from 1945 directed at stage actors[20]. This aesthetic device of "'[…] unmask[ing] the process of dramatic showing […]"'[21] becomes literally visible in Keaton's and Pirandello's works through the characters crossing the boundaries between the 'reality' of the film/play and the inner, dream-like/theatre-like plot.

In Keaton's *Sherlock Jr.* and *The Playhouse*, the characters' transgression produces a mainly comic effect as their becoming part of the inner story leads to confusion, and in *Sherlock Jr.* also to the usual chases. But more important here is Keaton's highly conscious and aesthetically most elaborate combination of cinematic and theatrical techniques. In *Sherlock Jr.*, Keaton's character steps into the film he's seeing in his dream, that is the dream's illusion, to free his girl. He does so just as he would step onto a stage, only to be pushed back by the villain into the film theatre, the dream's reality, and to immediately step into the fictional screen again. In *The Playhouse*, Keaton uses pieces of scenery which are being carried away around his character by stagehands to mark the transition from dream to illusion and, finally, to reality. The spectator becomes aware of the film's beginning being a dream when Keaton's character is shown asleep on a bed in what looks like a bedroom. Only when the stagehands remove the walls around him, does it become obvious that this is not supposed to be a real bedroom but merely scenery.

Similar to these films, Pirandello's two plays mentioned above show the characters on the first level step into and become part of the second plot. In *Sei Personaggi in Cerca d'Autore*, the family appearing "onstage" and interrupting the rehearsal process ask for an author to write their play so they are able to actually live their story: 'IL PADRE […]. Siamo qua in cerca d'un autore.'[22]. The characters in the 'Secondo Intermezzo Corale' ('Second Choral Interlude') in *Ciascuno a suo Modo* who are among the 'audience' on the first level seem to fuse with their representatives 'onstage' on the second level: 'LA MORENO. La mia stessa voce! I miei gesti! tutti i miei gesti! Mi sono vista! mi sono vista là!'[23] They go on to enact exactly the same scene presented before on the fictional stage.

As the examples demonstrate, the characters both of Pirandello's plays and Keaton's films are entangled in a process of representation that is unfolding on a stage/screen in the plot within the plot. By making the characters literally break the inner frame, Pirandello and Keaton each create a very different kind of comic. While with Pirandello the comic always contains a tragic note, Keaton makes even the characters' most serious mishaps appear comic. In both cases, however, it is the 'humoristic dissociation' resulting from the tragicomic opposition between being and appearing that most naturally provokes the audience's distance from the story – and thus their laughter.

II. Self-alienation in the process of artistic and social adaptation

Bertolt Brecht maintained that the use of *Verfremdung* naturally leads to the state of *Entfremdung*. According to his theory, the alienation of the individual in relation to the artistic work and, in a larger context, to the social environment inevitably entails the alienation of the individual from themselves. This double self-alienation is linked to the increasing loss of self in the modern world. It includes the self-alienation of the artist regarding their position in the process of artistic creation as well as that of the human being in general regarding their condition in a world of growing anonymity and enforced adaptation to mechanization.

1. The presence of the artist onstage and onscreen

At this point, it is essential to recall the special quality that lies in comparing two forms of art that are born out of and exist in different circumstances. Walter Benjamin states in his essay 'Das Kunstwerk im Zeitalter seiner technischen Reproduzierbarkeit'[24] (1936) that film, while destroying the non-recurring nature of everything that happens onscreen through reproducing it, is capable of bringing these occurrences closer to the audience. Thereby, film can establish a more intimate spatial and emotional relationship between the spectator and the events enacted onscreen[25]. Paradoxically, though, it is precisely the camera which, by irrevocably standing between performer and spectator, creates a distance between the two, just as it leads to a certain detachment on the part of the actor in relation to their role.

1.1. The relation of the artist to their work reflected in their self-perception

'*Der Schauspieler, der auf der Bühne agiert, versetzt sich in eine Rolle. Dem Filmdarsteller ist das sehr oft versagt.*'[26] As Benjamin explains, a film actor does not create and perceive their performance as a single, unitary act but as one being constituted of several autonomous elements, which is first and foremost due to the dependence on technical equipment[27]. This consideration must be taken into account when comparing Keaton's approach to creating comedy for the screen to modern European dramatists' theories on mise-en-scène and their use of theatrical devices on the stage.

The reflection necessary to simultaneously perceive and create 'the opposite', that is to undergo the process from 'un *avvertimento del contrario*' to 'il *sentimento del contrario*'[28], as Pirandello puts it, can happen only in the split personality of the comic artist. This double nature of the comedian is already philosophically defined by Charles Baudelaire in his essay 'De l'Essence du Rire' (1855) as '[…] l'existence d'une dualité permanente, la puissance d'être à la fois soi et un autre'[29]. While creating or enacting a comic situation, the comic artist must remain detached from this process: they must at once create the comic character and observe themselves in doing so. If the artist lacks this duality, the comic character/situation risks turning ridiculous. This appears even more relevant with regard to the art of silent performance where the artist has only visual elements at their disposal to arouse laughter.

Although in film the range for manipulation is far wider than in theatre, Keaton refused to resort to trickery which would lure the audience into an artificially created illusion. With his experience in stage acting, he knew exactly how to use the 'permanent duality' Baudelaire refers to. His improvisational manner of working out his films speaks to his highly visual imagination. Not overdoing the gag around which the story is built was Keaton's main concern, as Clyde Bruckman, the story writer for many of Keaton's films, remembers in Rudi Blesh's biography of Keaton: 'Buster was his own best gagman. He had judgment, taste; never overdid it, and never offended. He knew what was right for him.'[30] Keaton did, though, more than once rely on the audience's response: when, at a preview, they would not laugh at a scene he had intended to be funny, he would find another way of doing it or even omit it altogether. In his autobiography, Keaton recalls a scene in *The High Sign* (1921) he decided to alter after its failure at a preview[31] as well as a gag in *The Navigator* (1924) he canceled after realizing at the previews that it did not fit into the story line[32]. This approach was a remnant of the direct action-reaction principle common especially in American vaudeville around the turn of the twentieth century. At the time, performers used to put their trust in '"affective immediacy"'. Gags were literally tried out and then developped and refined '[…] depending upon the audience's reactions'[33]. It is from such experiences that Keaton learned that '"[t]he audience wants his comic to be human, not clever"'[34].

Although this kind of improvisation was no longer an acknowledged practice in the theatre of the twentieth century, Pirandello still returned to the idea of working in the style of the *commedia dell'arte* which enables the artist to '[…] revive the spontaneity and intelligence of improvisation […]'[35] through experiment. Despite giving precise stage directions concerning physical performance, even Samuel Beckett repeatedly included gags and comic surprises that might appear spontaneous and improvised. This is even more striking as these form a contrast to the seemingly somber atmosphere of his plays. One of the most illustrative examples can be found in *En attendant Godot* (1952) where Beckett incorporated a kind of comic interlude with the four characters interacting with each other almost in vaudeville-style.[36] All these various approaches require in equal parts involvement and detachment by the artist for the comic character/situation not to become ridiculous.

The relation of the artist to their work sometimes manifests itself more prominently through explicit self-reference. In the dream sequence of *The Playhouse*, Keaton employs a device applicable only in film: he sets up a performance in an opera house where everyone, that is actors, spectators and musicians, is played by Buster Keaton. The programme of 'Keaton's Opera House' reads 'Buster Keaton presents Buster Keaton's Minstrels', just as the 'Staff for Buster Keaton' consists of multiple Buster Keatons.[37] Before the show starts, one of the Keaton-spectators looks at the programme and says to his Keaton-wife: 'This Keaton fellow seems to be the whole show.'

Naming the artist behind the work is a method likewise used by Pirandello in some of his plays. In *Ciascuno a suo Modo*, he refers to himself in the meta-theatrical 'Premessa dell'Autore' ('Author's Preamble') before the beginning of the play: '[…] Pare che Pirandello abbia tratto l'argomento della sua nuova commedia *Ciascuno a suo modo*, che sarà rappresentata questa sera al Teatro …, dal suicidio drammaticissimo, avvenuto or è qualche mese a Torino, del giovine compianto scultore Giacomo La Vela.'[38] This notion of destroying any illusion by pointing out the creative thought behind the play is enhanced when 'audience-characters' of the frame plot comment in interludes on the performance presented onstage in the inner plot[39].

In some of his films, Buster Keaton uses more subtle means of hinting at the presence of the artist. Once more, these techniques are a reminiscence of his early days in vaudeville when, frequently, all members of the Keaton family appeared in identical outfits labeling them as The Three Keatons, The Four Keatons or The Five Keatons. Just as Charlie Chaplin is unmistakably recognizable merely through his outward appearance, the famous Keaton-hat is inextricably linked to Buster Keaton, drawing the spectator's attention to Keaton, the artist, who is both the creative mind behind the work and the actor in front of the camera. In combination with his stunts and gags, this accessory allows the comedian to remain Buster Keaton while representing a character. In more than one film, he makes the hat the centre of the comic action. In *Steamboat Bill, Jr.* (1928), his film father orders him to buy a new hat because he does not approve of his beret; in *The Navigator*, Keaton replaces his hat with a different one when it is blown from his head by the strong wind on the vessel.

Mentioning the artist by name and making visually fun of a prop closely linked to the artist are equally strong means of self-reference. Thus, both name and accessory become symbols of the artist's persona, making this specific persona remain present in the spectator's mind while they are watching him perform onscreen.

1.2. The split personality of actor and character leading to critical comment

The detachment of the actor in relation to the respective characters they are portraying is explored and exploited on an even more sophisticated level through the actor's concurrent multiple presence onscreen without their name being explicitly referred to. With this cinematic device, Buster

Keaton once more seems to visually anticipate an approach that Bertolt Brecht would later on lay down in a theory and refine for the stage.

Again, *The Playhouse* illustrates Keaton's artful play with the medium film. He puts on a minstrel show where he simultaneously portrays all nine participants in a group discussion on the stage of the playhouse. After that, he performs a short dance, with him dancing opposite himself. In this scene, the double presence is particularly accentuated by the 'two' dancers moving in synchrony. Another – though very different and even touching – example of the artist's multiple presence onscreen can be found in *The Cameraman*. The miniature double who acts alongside Keaton is not Keaton himself, but a little monkey, Josephine. Both Keaton and Josephine are identifiable as their mutual double by their identical caps. Additionally, the comedian and the monkey perform their gags with the same cleverness and dexterity. At the camera, Josephine is even more nimble than the original, Buster Keaton's character Shannon, grinding the camera like the little organ she used to grind in her former 'profession'. Interestingly, the first hint at the two characters' being their mutual double occurs at their very first meeting when Shannon overruns the monkey – just as he is constantly being overrun by everybody else.

According to Walter Benjamin, the aura of an actor, and with it the aura of the character they portray, exists only onstage and is lost in front of the camera as it depends on the actor's and spectators' being physically present at the same place at the same time.[40] This view is shared by Luigi Pirandello: the circumstances inherent in film make the actors feel as if in exile '"[…] non soltanto dal palcoscenico, ma quasi anche da se stessi. Perché la loro azione, l'azione *viva* del loro corpo *vivo*, là, sulla tela dei cinematografi, non c'è più: c'è *la loro immagine* soltanto, colta in un momento, in un gesto, in una espressione, che giuzza e scompare."'[41] To a certain degree, though, Keaton once more succeeds in bridging this gap between theatre and film by playing with the notions of the actor's/character's image and aura. In *The Cameraman*, the dual personality of the comic artist/character is personified in and through the little monkey, the mirror image of the comedian/character. The '"immagine muta"', the '"dumb image"', of the actor/character which appears as '"un' ombra inconsistente"', an '"unsubstantial phantom"'[42], becomes alive in this double presence. The one who perceives and the one who is perceived are both parts of the actor and, in this case, also of the character. They enact for and interact with each other, thus becoming at once performers and their mutual audience. In *The Playhouse*, Keaton goes even further. By portraying the entire cast onstage and every spectator in the audience, showing countless versions of himself, he basically deconstructs the notion of the actor's/character's aura.

According to Bertolt Brecht, the actor must by no means be confounded with their role[43]. Acting is no longer considered a process of identification but one of showing a performance. In his essay 'Was ist Episches Theater? [Erste Fassung]', Benjamin quotes Brecht's postulate:

> Der Schauspieler muss eine Sache zeigen, und er muss sich zeigen. Er zeigt die Sache natürlich, indem er sich zeigt, und er zeigt sich, indem er die Sache zeigt. Obwohl dies zusammenfällt, darf es doch nicht so zusammenfallen, dass der Gegensatz (Unterschied) zwischen diesen beiden Aufgaben verschwindet.[44]

Brecht calls for an acting style in the manner of the famous street scene, where a person recounts an accident by demonstrating the event and rendering the dialogue in the past tense and in the third person. Neither the accident's witness nor the bystanders listening to the account must identify with the event and the people involved. On the stage of the epic theatre, this technique not only introduces a completely new aesthetic, but also creates a critical distance preventing the actor and the audience from emotionally identifying with the plot and its characters.[45]

Theatre, though, was not alone in using meta-theatrical means to show the actor's relation to their character in a new light. In *Sherlock Jr.*, Keaton plays with the notion of critical distance in a most refined manner. At the end of the film, Keaton's character, the projectionist, is reunited with his girl. Yet, he does not know how to proceed in showing his affection for her. Carefully watching the film he is presenting, he literally quotes and even copies the gestures the male character is enacting 'for him' on 'his' screen. As if in rehearsal, he meticulously follows the man's movements one by one. This performance by Keaton reminds of two main aspects of the epic theatre: that it is essential '"Gesten zitierbar zu machen"'[46] and that gesture exists '[…] je häufiger wir einen Handelnden unterbrechen'[47]. In the scene just described, the actor is portraying a character who is imitating someone he is watching while he, the actor, is being watched by us, the audience. Through this complex combination, the artist as well as that audience gain a critical distance. This distance inevitably makes the spectator pass their critical judgment on the character's behaviour. With Keaton, of course, critical comment always means laughter.

In the film *Film*[48], written by Samuel Beckett in 1963 and filmed in 1965 with Buster Keaton in the leading role, the phenomenon of the split identity is complicated by the motif of the gaze, visually symbolized by Keaton's eyes. The motto of this short piece is *'Esse est percipi'* ('to be is to be perceived'), which reflects the dichotomy of being and perceiving on the one hand and of being perceived on the other. The shot of Keaton's eye at the beginning of the film translates this motto into a metaphor: returning the gaze here becomes a threat. O, the main character, is called 'object', where as E, the camera, is the 'eye'. In reality, though, O is both subject in that it is and perceives and object in that it is perceived. O tries to evade any gaze, no matter if it comes from other human beings, from animals, or from photographs. The patch covering one of his eyes reflects this fear of being seen as well as his refusal to see himself. E, the camera, follows O, yet never discovers his face – this happens only at the end of the film. It is then that O can no longer avoid looking at himself. Perceiving himself through E and being thus perceived by the camera and the spectator coincide. O's only escape consists in covering his face with his hands, virtually hiding from the spectator's view and his own. In doing so, he almost explicitly denies Brecht's demand that the actor 'show himself'. At the same time, though, it seems as if Beckett's film amplifies and unites two images from Keaton's film, *Sherlock Jr*, made forty years earlier: the split personality shown in the protagonist's body stepping out of his real body at the beginning of the dream sequence and the gaze the protagonist is directing at the screen – and at us – at the end of the film while we, the audience, are watching him.

It is clear, then, that the split personality of the actor is always tied to the gaze: the actor's gaze at themselves (and at times also at the spectators) as well as the audience's gaze at the actor. It is this interconnection that makes the aesthetic distance literally visible, naturally leading both the actor and the spectator to adopt a critical attitude. Whereas Keaton first and foremost aims at laughter, only implicitly pointing out social injustice, modern European dramatists prioritize social and existential questions over the comic effect, as will be demonstrated in the second part of this chapter.

2. The self-alienation of the character through their confrontation with the surrounding world

In many of his films, Buster Keaton addressed the issue of identity. Although employing traditional vaudeville techniques such as role play and confusion, he did not rely on them as ends in themselves. In his hands, they became means that helped him raise questions equally being discussed by contemporary philosophers and dramatists like Henri Bergson and Bertolt Brecht. A few decades later, it was Eugène Ionesco, in particular, who would elaborate on topics such as the individual's loss of identity and their subsequent transformation through virtually verbalizing classic vaudeville techniques.

2.1. The perception of identity and the character's transformation into a persona

Approaching the issue of identity, especially with regard to the character's confrontation with the surrounding world, needs to take into account two fundamental and interrelated aspects: the perception of a character by other characters and the creation of a persona through the character themselves. This dual approach does not reflect the dichotomy of the character's appearing versus their being as creating a persona means conscious transformation by the character, and not the character's mere condition of being.

In numerous comedies, Buster Keaton relies on comic techniques and narrative gags like chases, mistaken identity and role-playing that often result in utter confusion, as is typical of farces. Another comic effect is achieved through what Henri Bergson describes in his essay 'Le Rire' (1900) as the comic characters' *'insociabilité'* ('unsociability') and *'immorailité'* ('immorality')[49]. Their anomalous nature manifests itself in their equally anomalous behaviour that breaks the firm frame formed by society, history and tradition. It is this clash between reality and ideal in '[...] la "contradizione" fondamentale, a cui si suol dare per causa principale il disaccordo che il sentimento e la meditazione scoprono o fra la vita reale e l'ideale umano o fra le nostre aspirazioni e le nostre debolezze e miserie [...]'[50]. The contradiction between the socially and morally ideal image of the human being and the individual's real nature is, of course, the most classic feature of comedy. In order to represent this confrontation in a comic manner, the dramatist/filmmaker chooses between two patterns, as Gerald Mast explains: the play/film either upholds the values and assumptions of society, urging the comic character to reform their ways and conform to social expectations, or it maintains that the comic character's antisocial behaviour is superior to the norms set by society.[51]

Mast states in his chapter on Buster Keaton that '[t]he elements surrounding Keaton is not society [...] as in Chaplin's films, but nature itself [...]'[52]. This, however, is not completely true. Although many of the Keaton-characters are fighting against nature, other examples show that social status occasionally is an element of conflict in his films. Keaton does not remain in the domain of the usual contrast between being and appearing. In most of his films, the girl he wants to marry sets conditions he has to fulfill before being accepted by her. The existence of his comic character is never guaranteed on its own terms, but is tied to his failure to meet the expectations of society. As Herbert Read argues in his essay 'Rational Society and Irrational Art', human imagination mostly '[...] struggles to idealize [the fellow human being] and unify [...]'[53] this ideal with reality, which means it sees the fellow human being as somebody they are not. It is this gap that essentially creates the comic character.

Also, the Keaton-character is, in one way or another, always at the margin of society as he usually does not conform to any of its expectations and values. In *The General* (1927), for example, his character, Johnny Gray, has to prove that he is a brave soldier defending and protecting his country in order to be 'worth' the girl and her family. The initial gag is, of course, that he does apply for being enlisted but is sent back on the grounds that he is more valuable to the country as an engineer on the train. Likewise, in *The Cameraman*, Shannon's obvious clumsiness at handling a camera excludes him from the community he most wishes to belong to. The end, though, shows him as a most accomplished man in his field, now outdoing his colleagues with his skills.

In modern European theatre, the issues of perception and transformation have farther-reaching consequences that are also considerably more serious than in Keaton's films and not seldom even tragic. Society does not always outright reject the character who does not fit into its ideological system; even worse, it often transforms a human being. Bertolt Brecht's play *Mann ist Mann*[54] deals with this phenomenon in a particularly explicit way. Written in 1926 and rewritten in 1938, it is a response to contemporary political circumstances in Germany (reflected by changes Brecht made in the 1930s) and testament to Brecht's serious intentions behind the drama's comic nature. At its heart, it decries man's being subject to forces surrounding them – moral, social as well as political ones. In a 'Zwischenspruch' ('Interlude') that serves as meta-theatrical comment, the widow Begbick says:

Herr Brecht: Mann ist Mann.

[…]

Aber Herr Brecht beweist auch dann

dass man mit einem Menschen beliebig viel machen kann.

[…]

Dem Mann wird menschlich nähergetreten

Er wird mit Nachdruck ohne Verdruss gebeten

Sich dem Laufe der Welt schon anzupassen

Und seinen Privatfisch schwimmen zu lassen.

[…][55]

In order to meet established moral, social and political standards, man is forced to renounce their own personality and create a persona, to literally play a role. It is this struggle to live up to these demands that Keaton, too, addresses in his films (even if not as vehemently as Chaplin does). But whereas his protagonist, while adapting to and even being able to profit from any given circumstance, always remains true to himself and most times retains the upper hand, in modern European theatre, the characters at the margin of society either remain excluded or are forced to adapt, thereby losing their individuality.

Keaton's film *Cops*, in particular, addresses the question of what constitutes the 'ideal' human being in a society. Once more, Buster tries to become someone he is not, in this case a successful businessman. In his attempt to transform himself, though, he cannot escape his own self. In this film, the contrast between the real and the 'ideal' individual, while still creating humour, makes very clear that comedy can never exist without the tragic. *Cops*, in fact, is one of the rare examples where the outcome for the hero is not a happy one: he is chased by the whole apparatus of the police force and finally caught by it.

What, in Buster Keaton's film, is first and foremost a presentation through purely visual means, becomes a metaphor in Brecht's theatre where the issue of social and political ideology constitutes his plays' core. The attitude of modern man Terry Hodgson calls 'pessimism about human relations'[56] is only one element among many in Keaton's films, but becomes an acute topic in twentieth-century European drama. In a society that imposes strict social, political and ideological norms, characters are forced to play double roles to fit into this society. The situation is frequently aggravated by extreme circumstances. In Bertolt Brecht's *Mutter Courage und ihre Kinder*[57], it is war that leads the mother to try to '[...] établir un compromis entre le raisonnable et l'irrationnel [...]'[58]. In order to regain her integrity, she is forced to engage in duplicity, thus creating a persona within the boundaries of the given social environment. In Pirandello's plays, by contrast, there is no compromise for the characters: they remain themselves, that is *personaggi* who retain all their inner contradictions.[59]

The comic effect in Keaton's films arises from the confrontation between his character's confidence in his abilities and a reality that puts these very abilities to the test. Again, Keaton used a technique that was popular in vaudeville: the art of mimicry. He drew from his early experiences onstage when, as a little child, he learned to imitate every movement and spoken word he witnessed in the performances of his father and other actors. This made the audience perceive '[...] him as a distorted double image of his father, almost like a funhouse mirror come to life'[60]. While Keaton's silent film comedies show his character's constant, but mostly vain attempts to adapt to and imitate his social environment, in modern drama, imitation means complete transformation of the character, almost down to self-denial. For Bertolt Brecht, theatre was, above all, an expression of political commitment. He especially elaborated on the phenomenon of the individual's being shaped by their social and political environment which he always saw as a logical consequence of historical development. Therefore, all human behaviour must be recognized as a '"variable of the milieu"'[61] and cannot be interpreted strictly as alienation from the self, but rather as a natural given in the historical and social sense.[62]

While Keaton remains essentially comic, the aim of politically committed playwrights at the time and later on was to create plays that attacked politics, social order and art designed only to please. By presenting and criticizing contemporary conditions and constraints, they introduced a new form of theatre, which subsequently grew into existentialist and absurd drama. Over the course of the century, this new form would evolve into the 'Théâtre engagé', theatre committed to social and political issues.

2.2. Enforced integration through physical and verbal mechanization

According to Henri Bergson, the comic character displays one major typical feature: '[…] *ce corps nous fait penser à une simple mécanique* […]'[63]. The act of transforming oneself and of being transformed by society is, as shown earlier, a question of sharing the so-called rationality of an allegedly coherent social body. This issue was explored not only by Brecht, but also by dramatists of the Theatre of the Absurd like, for example, Eugène Ionesco who frequently presented the process of transformation as a process of mechanization in its various forms.

Although the aspect of the human condition in the modern world does not, at first sight, seem to have been Buster Keaton's main concern, it is, as analyzed beforehand, at least the starting point in most of his films and the basic issue in *Cops*.[64] To convey his character's confrontation with the environment, Keaton again relies on the visual impact – mostly resulting from physical performance, highly choreographed scenes and the use of the frame. It is through these devices that he achieves effects similar to those created by Bertolt Brecht in *Mann ist Mann* and Eugène Ionesco in *Jacques ou La Soumission* (1953)[65]. Most scenes in *Cops* present Buster Keaton as the alien element in the scenery. In one scene, he travels with his horse and carriage packed with furniture in the middle of a formation of policemen marching in step. Then, he unintentionally causes an explosion by throwing a fuse. A few moments later, a street is shown empty; suddenly, a single man – Keaton's character –, small against the immense background of New York's houses, comes running around the corner as he is being chased by hundreds of policemen. Here, Keaton displays his mastery of meticulously combining individual and collective movement. In addition, the long shot, along with the use of the immobile frame, emphasizes the visual and metaphorical contrast between the individual human body and the collective body of policemen. It is this combination of choreography and mise-en-scène that creates an unusual visual harmony. It also documents Keaton's assertion that the silent film comedian, in particular, has to stick to precise, even mathematical calculation in order to achieve exact timing[66]. Ultimately, in his attempt to become part of one collective body, in this case the business world, Keaton's character inevitably ends up fleeing another collective body, that of the police force, and getting caught up by it. His fate has become '[…] fate washed out through the machine-like hostility of man towards his fellow man'[67]. In this respect, it is worth noting Walter Kerr's claim that, in comparison with Charlie Chaplin, '[…] Keaton's was the purer use of the [comic] form […]' as '[…] there was no admixture of sentiment, no bid for pathos […]'[68].

Brecht, for his part, builds on the idea of mechanization, transforming it into a metaphor both through verbal and, at times, even purely visual means. In *Mann ist Mann*, he hides the transformation of the main character, Galy Gay, from the spectators' view by surrounding him with the play's other characters. The moment the circle of human bodies around Gay opens up, it is evident that he has lost his individuality and become part of a collective body:

Die Soldaten bringen die Sachen, bilden einen Kreis um Galy Gay, so daß er dem
Publikum verdeckt ist. Während dieser Zeit spielt die Musik den Kriegsmarsch [...].

Die Soldaten öffnen den Kreis [...] Galy Gay in der Mitte, von Waffen starrend, ein
Messer zwischen den Zähnen [...].[69]

Visually, the surprise effect is similar to the one achieved by Keaton at the end of *Cops* when his character opens the gates of the police station and is taken in by the policemen. Thematically and metaphorically, though, Gay's transformation has far more serious implications. Whereas the Keaton-character makes a conscious decision to let himself be caught by the police force, yet without really becoming part of their collective body, Gay's decision to become a soldier means losing his identity as an individual and being transformed into a part of the human war machine.

The menacing force emanating from an entity that is composed of individuals who have lost their individuality is, in Eugène Ionesco's plays, no longer expressed through images but language, specifically through the use of mechanistic language. Gradually, the characters give up their free will and submit to the irrationality of their surrounding world. In his 'comédie naturaliste' (literally translated 'naturalistic comedy'), *Jacques ou la Soumision*, this mechanization of spoken language functions as allegedly rational force society uses to subdue the allegedly irrational rebellion of the main character. At the beginning of the play, Jacques's resistance manifests itself in his refusal to talk at all. When he does express his opinion, he does so only to contradict his family. They, in turn, serve as a symbol of the so-called 'normality' that is based on the most abstruse conversations. It is only after Jacques relinquishes his stubbornness towards the system and repeats

comme un automate
J'adore les pommes de terre au lard!
J'adore les pommes de terre au lard!
J'adore les pommes de terre au lard![70]

that his mother says to her husband: 'Gaston, dans ce cas-là, si l'en est ainsi, on pourrait le marier! [...]'[71] which eventually leads to the son's getting integrated into society.

Both Buster Keaton and twentieth-century European dramatists use the human body and/or language as vehicles to depict and respond to the condition of man in the modern world, thereby demonstrating that the allegedly rational order imposed on the individual by a powerful collective body is a pure construct of the human mind. The collective mask is enforced upon each member of society; they cannot exist without this mask.[72] While the process of a character's transformation might provoke laughter on the part of the audience, they still come to realize that the outcome for the character is tragic as they lose their autonomy and with it their individuality. In this paradox lies the tragicomic power of these works.

III. Between traditional performance techniques and modern concerns: man's confrontation with the animate and inanimate world

Relating Buster Keaton's concepts and aesthetics exclusively with modern European theatre would mean ignoring that many of his ideas and devices also bear a strong resemblance to specific characteristics already established in literature and drama during the age of European Romanticism. In the 'Préface de Cromwell' to his play *Cromwell* (1827), Victor Hugo advocates a form of drama that breaks with the concept of Classicism: nature no longer reflects the elements' existing in harmony but in confrontation with each other.[73] In a larger sense, then, the world in general – and man in particular – consists of conflicting elements, too. This new ontological and ideological view entails a new aesthetic postulating that representation of the comic must not exclude the tragic – and vice versa. On the contrary, they elucidate each other. The beautiful and the ugly, the grotesque and the sublime, all of which Hugo equates with comedy and tragedy, are now necessary components of drama.[74] These are recurring pairings in Keaton's films and twentieth-century European theatre alike.

1. The integration of the human body into the animate/inanimate world

One of the main motifs in Buster Keaton's films is man's position and role within the animate and inanimate world. He expresses his characters' relationship to their environment almost exclusively through physical performance that, in turn, is accentuated by a sophisticated mise-en-scène, thereby again creating strong visual effects. His manifold approaches to integrating the human body into nature and/or the material and technological world provides his films and characters with a tragicomic note. The adventures and mishaps may have serious implications for Keaton's characters, yet they are intended to provoke laughter on the part of the audience. The topic of the human body's being integrated into the animate or inanimate world in one way or another would be increasingly explored in modern European theatre as well, even though in a completely different manner. What film and drama share is their concern with the growing gap between what is still subordinate to the power and will of man and what man has to submit to.

1.1. Staging the human body as object/instrument

Most important in this context is Keaton's use of space and of the actor's position within the frame. It testifies to a serious concern that had become predominant in virtually all art movements since the beginning of the twentieth century. In a world of advancing mechanization, man had to cope with more than inter-human relationships. On the screen as well as on the stage, the loss of man's alleged central ontological status in the universe was symbolized by the active human body's being increasingly made and presented as equal to all the other elements surrounding it.

30

Using the human body as an object or instrument and bringing it in tune with props was a common vaudeville technique. The performers' skills at handling the inanimate and the animate were the main visual attractions of this theatrical form. They also constituted the principal features in the Act of The Three Keatons. Buster Keaton describes these early childhood experiences in the first chapters of his autobiography.[75] In The Keatons's Act, a broom, a table, and the child Buster Keaton were the focus of attention. In one gag, Keaton's father was 'wiping up the floor with [him]', using his son as '"The Human Mop"'.[76] In many of his films, Buster Keaton draws on this tradition, transforming his body into a prop. One example can be found in a scene from *Cops* where his character is driving through the city on a carriage that is being pulled by a horse and packed with furniture all of which he has accidentally become the owner. Feeling bored by the long journey, he lies down to sleep. A long shot shows the virtually driverless carriage with the man being asleep and the furniture piled up behind him. It seems as if Keaton had become one of the furniture pieces, being just as inert as they are. Whereas, in this scene, the body is a neutral element like all the others, a sense of the body's alienation from itself arises as soon as it is forced to turn itself into an instrument, thereby losing its human characteristics. This happens in *The Navigator* when Keaton's character, Rollo, realizes that he and his girl are in great danger of being captured by the cannibals. He turns his body into a raft for the girl so they both manage to get away from the island and reach safety on the vessel. The impression of the body's becoming a mechanical instrument is visually emphasized through Keaton's diving suit which disguises his human shape and makes his movements appear like those of a robot.

The two scenes perfectly illustrate that, in Buster Keaton's films, the human body never loses its natural shape completely, no matter to what degree it appears to be integrated into the immediate surroundings. Resorting to ancient vaudeville techniques, Keaton transforms them by transferring them into a modern thematic and artistic context. Twentieth-century European dramatists would take a much more radical approach, both in theory and in practice. The integration of the human body into these new contexts would be reflected first and foremost in physical and verbal performances breaking with rules that had reigned on the stage for centuries.

Buster Keaton visualizes the body's integration into space by showing physical performance literally from a new perspective. As Robert Knopf explains in detail, '[…] long shots emphasize the body in space', thereby making the actor's physical performance the focus of the spectator's attention.[77] The individual is presented as being in a constant struggle either to fit into or escape from an environment that appears more and more menacing. One of the most obvious examples of this struggle can be found in *The Navigator*. The absurdity of man's effort to gain control over their mechanized environment is symbolized in the visual contrast between the small, fragile human bodies on one side and the gigantic vessel on the other. Once more, it is this juxtaposition of opposites that creates the comic impression, as in the scene where Rollo and his girl are running along the deck while involuntarily keeping the same distance from each other, so that they never meet. Through the use of the long shot, their movements are emphasized so as to make the characters resemble mechanized parts of their environment rather than two human bodies acting in a natural way.

It seems not exactly appropriate to equate space as used by Keaton with that Antonin Artaud describes in *Le Théâtre et son Double* (1931) with reference to the stage. Artaud defines space as '[…] un lieu physique et concret qui demande qu'on le remplisse, et qu'on lui fasse parler son langage concret'[78]. Space plays the major role in expressing contacts, conflicts, thoughts and feelings in the most concrete and even sensual way. Likewise, language is no longer a language of words, but a material language that consists of everything present onstage and that first and foremost appeals to the senses, not to the mind[79]. In this concept, therefore, 'la poésie de langage', the poetry of language and words, is replaced with 'une poésie dans l'espace', a poetry in space.[80] It should be noted here that Artaud advocated a return to ancient forms of theatre and performance and that he was particularly influenced by Balinese theatre.

Buster Keaton was one of the most skillful artists when it came to adapting elements from vaudeville to the new artistic language of cinema. It was the combination of traditional performance techniques and a mise-en-scène relying precisely on the technical advances made around the turn of the twentieth century that allowed him to articulate man's ever more fragile position in the modern world. Whereas Keaton ridicules the new reality of the individual's increasingly being lost, Artaud chooses a far more radical and darker approach, turning the theatrical representation into an end in itself. His concept of mise-en-scène, therefore, requires a form of language that disrupts all traditional relationships between man and the spoken word as well as between man and the space surrounding them.

1.2. Bringing physical performance and the inanimate in tune

Just as he integrates the human body into the world around it, Keaton frequently animates these environments to make them fit in seamlessly with his physical performance. Often, his character's actions spring from necessity or even a need for survival, forcing him to alienate either his own body from itself or the objects around him from their essential nature. In adapting his physical performance to the surroundings and vice versa, Keaton creates the visual impression of a harmonious interaction between the human body and the inanimate world.

At times, Keaton's characters are confronted with a technological environment that compels them to adapt so as not to lose control. In *The General*, the protagonist Johnnie Gray performs his duties on the train with the same dispassionate accuracy as does the machinery around him. His persistence in performing these mechanical movements in tune with the surrounding technical equipment is comic as it reveals what Henri Bergson calls '[…] une substitution quelconque de l'artificiel au naturel'[81]. That is to say the comic results from the contrast of the unnatural being imposed onto the natural while the human body is being presented as if acting in harmony with the machinery surrounding it. This device is one important element of farce, the basis of vaudeville, where characters often are types whose movements do no longer represent individual human actions.

In hist first manifesto of 'Le Théâtre de la Cruauté' (1932), Artaud declares that

> [l]'acteur est à la fois un élément de première importance, puisque c'est de l'efficacité de son jeu que dépend la réussite du spectacle, et une sorte d'élément passif et neutre, puisque toute initiative personnelle lui est rigoureusement refusée.[82]

The dichotomy of activity and passivity on the part of the actor as described by Artaud is an element equally in Keaton's performance in *The General*, even if not as radically exploited. As actor, he is consciously using his body as an instrument in that he is deliberately subordinating it to the rhythm of the machinery around him. This, in turn, makes his character's movements appear as if in interaction with technology, whereas, in reality, they are rather a reaction or an enforced adaptation to it. Yet, in Keaton's case, the transformation of the human body and with it the body's alienation from itself can never go as far as in Artaud's concept regarding the use of the human body. With Artaud, the actor is at once an active and a passive element of the performance. As the human body is no longer integrated into but rather amalgamated with its surroundings, the animate and inanimate fuse. Theatrical performance becomes, above all, a symbolical and metaphysical act.

Despite Artaud's and Keaton's different approaches to the act of performing, both artists redefine the relationship between actor and space, with the human body becoming a mere instrument. For Artaud, the actor is, in a metaphysical sense, the living embodiment of the dichotomy of activity and passivity. The actor Keaton, though, as the scene from *The General* demonstrates, retains his full autonomy. This, in turn, enables Keaton to allow his protagonist to adapt – to some degree – to the technological world around him, so that he, too, maintains at least part of his autonomy. This leads him to exploit both body and technology to face a dangerous situation and survive.

It was not only his physical skills, though, which made Keaton a distinguished performer, but also his ingenuity in adapting objects to his artistic purposes. He did not merely use them, but, as Clyde Bruckman claims, '"[…] he makes things alive […]"'[83]. Again, the interaction between the inanimate world and the actor's body was a tradition stemming from the vaudeville stage where it was common for the characters to transform things, so that they did eventually serve their intentions. In Keaton's films, this way of acting reflects a rather naïve confidence of the Keaton-character in himself, in his abilities to cope with the oddities of life, but also in the inanimate world and its reliability. Yet, his naïvety is also pragmatic. This may well mean assigning objects a function different from their original one. In *The Playhouse*, after flooding the stage and the orchestra pit, Keaton's character tries to flee the theatre's manager by using a drum as a boat and a violin as a paddle, adapting himself to the circumstances as well as the circumstances to his needs. Another example of Keaton's inventiveness can be found in the dream sequence of *Sherlock Jr.*. Stopped abruptly in front of a lake during the final chase, the car's upper part with the two passengers inside lands on the water. In order to keep the car afloat, Keaton transforms it into a boat by raising its convertible like a sail.

Keaton's instinctive approach to employing props as comedy material is impressively explained in Kevin Brownlow's and David Gill's documentary *Buster Keaton – A Hard Act to Follow*[84]. His use of tricks and stunts in combination with animating the inanimate presented an image of man and the world unseen until then since, with him, the animated object became an almost inseparable part of both. Even though Keaton followed his intuition in adapting his performance to the given circumstances of a location and in exploiting them, there are striking affinities to the theory Artaud formulated in the 1930s. Artaud calls for a similar transformation of objects and even for a form of anarchy that challenges all conventional connections between objects[85]. This might well – or should – mean assigning these objects a new purpose. They are to be taken out of their original contexts and used in ways not corresponding to their essential nature while still retaining their relation to the human body[86].

There are also some surprising parallels between Keaton's and Eugène Ionesco's approach to the use of objects. Although in the French playwright's works verbal language constitutes the main theatrical tool, he does not exclude the 'primitive' kind of performance, either, accepting only those constraints that the theatre stage by its very nature imposes on a mise-en-scène. He even advocates a circus-style use of props.[87] Ionesco explains this form of interplay between the actor and the inanimate in his *Notes et Contre-Notes*:

> Il est [...] non seulement permis, mais recommandé de faire jouer les accessoires, faire vivre les objets, animer les décors, concrétiser les symboles.
>
> De même que la parole est continuée par le geste, le jeu, la pantomime, qui, au moment où la parole devient insuffisante, se substituent à elle, les éléments scéniques matériels peuvent l'amplifier à leur tour.[88]

Remarkably, then, modern European drama increasingly allowed or even required objects to virtually become alive and gradually replace language, especially as words were no longer adequate for expressing man's condition in the modern world. In silent film comedy, by contrast, it was the absence of spoken language in the first place that naturally emphasized the visual impact of the interplay between actor and objects. The new theatrical freedom to experiment with the inanimate that was taking hold on the twentieth-century European stage was certainly inspired by the visual imagination of film artists like Buster Keaton.

2. Man's loss of control over the surrounding world

Often enough, though, man's surrounding world – be it the natural elements or the mechanized environment – does not submit to their will. In Keaton's films, it is when man's will encounters an adverse reality that the comic loses its pure nature and becomes more ambiguous. In extreme cases, the comic hero finds himself in even nightmarish or anarchic situations. In contrast to Keaton's works, the plays of the Theatre of the Absurd do not remain in the here and now. While still drawing on elements of farce and vaudeville, they not only display an absurd and grotesque nature, but also an increasingly fantastic and anarchic side verging on the apocalyptic, with the individual being thrown back on their own resources.

2.1. Absurdity and anarchy as expressed in mise-en-scène

Whenever a character both in Keaton's comedies and the plays of the Theatre of the Absurd is facing a hostile environment, existence becomes a struggle. Yet, comparing Buster Keaton with a playwright like Samuel Beckett reveals that they ground this struggle in completely different realities: while Keaton's characters are confronted with a nature that is still intact, in Beckett's plays there is no nature anymore to be confronted with. Despite this fundamental difference, both the motif of nature's presence in Keaton's films as well as that of nature's absence in Beckett's plays are closely linked to an 'absurd' language of mise-en-scène. At times, Buster Keaton even comes close to Antonin Artaud's anarchic language of performance, even though their works display dramatic realities that cannot be compared.

Often, it is the notion of nature's violence that is important in Keaton's films. This violence can become manifest in natural conditions dangerous in themselves which the hero has to face. Keaton repeatedly uses water – be it in the form of a rainstorm in *Steamboat Bill, Jr.*, a bursting fish tank in *The Playhouse*, a lake in *The Cameraman* and *Sherlock Jr.*, a wild river in *Our Hospitality*, or even the ocean in *The Navigator* that turn threatening – to depict the individual's place in an untamed environment. It is true that this approach still reflects the traditional, rather romantic view of nature's simply being stronger than man. At the same time, it is the way Keaton presents this relationship between the human being and nature that allows a comparison with later European theatre. As he recalls in his autobiography, he generally developped his gags based on the local conditions of the actual environment where he was shooting his films: '[…] I always preferred working on location because more good gags suggested themselves in new and unfamiliar surroundings.'[89] Relying on the background of an existing landscape, Keaton nevertheless succeeds in creating quite a fantastic atmosphere. Robert Knopf explains the ambiguous connection between Keaton's physical performance and his utilizing the frame that defines the filmic presentation of his gags. Even though Knopf's analysis refers to the artist's ability to play with the mechanistic world, it can equally be applied to Keaton's approach to exploiting natural environments. His '[…] use of long shots accentuates the spectacular, irrational functioning of his […] world while his insistence on maintaining the "integrity of his performance" keeps his spectacle grounded in reality'[90]. This kind of mise-en-scène also helps Keaton create a sharp contrast between the vast and powerful world surrounding the characters on one side and their small and vulnerable bodies on the other. In *Our Hospitality*, for example, Keaton and his girl are shown being carried away by a wild river while fleeing the girl's father and brothers. The rapids are of enormous, yet still natural dimensions. As the characters are not able to gain control over their environment, they must find ways to adapt to the challenges they are confronted with in order to survive.

In the Theatre of the Absurd, cruelty of nature takes on an entirely different form: it consists in a complete absence of nearly all natural elements. As Martin Esslin explains in his 'Introduction' to *The Theatre of the Absurd*, the term 'absurd' describes a state of being '"out of harmony with reason or propriety; incongruous, unreasonable, illogical"'[91]. Its dimension does not only seem to transcend human understanding but any universal order. Samuel Beckett's plays, in particular, show the condition of man after the final big storm when virtually all palpable surroundings have disappeared. A tree in *En Attendant Godot*, a heap of earth in *Happy Days* (1961) and memories of an intact nature as recalled in *Krapp's Last Tape* (1958) and in the conversation between Nagg and Nell in *Fin de Partie* (1957) are the only shadows of a past intact. The rest has been destroyed or has simply vanished, be it through natural disaster or the destructive behaviour of mankind. As '[l]a nature nous a oubliés' or as '[i]l n'y a plus de nature'[92], there is nothing more to face than existence itself, making the characters painfully aware of their own selves.

In Keaton's films and Beckett's plays, the characters' loss of control over their surroundings is closely tied to the shape of the respective environment they encounter. As Keaton's characters still struggle to survive hostile conditions posed by the outside world, their view and actions are always directed outward and aiming for a lucky outcome. With Beckett, the characters, having already lost this fight, are largely resigned to their fate and looking inward, with only little hope for a fortunate turn of events.

In some of his films, Keaton takes the comic hero's confrontation with the outside world a step further, up to the point where it is no longer possible for his character to adapt to an inanimate world that has gained an autonomy of its own. The situation becomes even more complex and, at times, dangerous for him when the inanimate world itself loses its autonomy and is being subjected to the forces of nature. In these moments, the character's experiences turn into a nightmare, sometimes resembling a state of complete anarchy. Just as Buster Keaton makes the inanimate world submit to his character's will, in more than one comedy he makes human inventiveness turn against man. The house that Keaton's character builds in *One Week* displays a completely irrational structure when finished, with its distorted lines and angles reminding of Expressionism. The front door is on the first floor, leading outside from the bathroom to nowhere; the kitchen sink is built on the outer wall of the ground floor, part of which proves to be revolving when Keaton turns it around to enter the house; the window and the porch are absurdly contorted. His character has become a victim of his own 'capabilities' as he can no longer adapt to an environment he himself has created. Yet, he does not understand or recognize his failure, instead assigning the house an autonomy that is more powerful than his rational thinking or will. The comic gets a darker touch when nature and the inanimate surroundings get out of control simultaneously, which happens in the storm scene in the same film. The house starts spinning like a merry-go-round gone wild that Keaton's character is unable to stop. The people inside are whirled around like tops and finally blown out of the house one after another. The situation has turned into a grotesque nightmare. A similar scene occurs in *Steamboat Bill, Jr.* when a heavy rainstorm and an ensuing flood transform objects and human beings into mere playthings. As Robert Knopf argues, '[...] despite the scholars' claims for Keaton's classicism, the climactic sequences of his films overreach classicism, resulting in spectacular displays that can only be called "excess"'[93]. It is for scenes like these that Keaton created an almost anarchic visual language.

An even more radical kind of 'excess', while also encompassing highly surreal elements, was first introduced into theatre by the playwright and theorist Alfred Jarry at the end of the nineteenth century. In his approach to the art of mise-en-scène, he advocated a chaotic dramatic reality utterly opposed to any logic and any naturalistic kind of representation. Keaton's scenes depicting an environment uncontrollable by man reveal a strikingly similar irrationality. At the same time, their visual rendering seems to already represent the 'negation of the theory of gravity' that, in modern European theatre, accounts for 'the meaninglessness of human progress'[94]. Artaud, in particular, lamented the state of contemporary theatre:

> Le théâtre contemporain est en décadence parce qu'il a perdu le sentiment d'un côté du sérieux et de l'autre du rire. Parce qu'il a rompu avec la gravité, avec l'efficacité immédiate et pernicieuse – et pour tout dire avec le Danger.
>
> Parce qu'il a perdu d'autre part le sens de l'humour vrai et du pouvoir de dissociation physique et anarchique du rire.[95]

In response to the perceived shortcomings, he developped Jarry's concept further, conceiving a language of performance intended to not only reflect irrationality turned into madness, but to also convey the impact of this madness on man. As a result, physicality becomes the most essential and most radical part of performance, allowing the artist '[…] to deform reality for purely formal ends […]'[96]. The immediacy of the physical experience is meant to make violence and cruelty literally being felt by both actors and spectators during the representation, yet not necessarily and exclusively in the form of physical pain. Rather, it is the mere presence of bodies and objects onstage that has to be so intense for everyone involved in the theatrical event to feel them physically and mentally. Again, the act of performing as well as the act of watching should not remain an immanent experience, but should extend into the metaphysical realm. This can most effectively be achieved with all theatrical conventions being abandoned and the sense of unpredictability, chaos and danger reigning supreme. Artaud concludes that only anarchy constitutes the true stage language and also gives laughter back its essence.[97]

Keaton's scenes of 'excess' reflect and respond to a world that man has begun to experience as increasingly being beyond their control. Again, it is this unequal confrontation between the individual and their hostile surroundings that creates the tragicomic nature of these scenes and that finds its expression in a physically almost violent language of performance. Even though Buster Keaton never leaves the immanent reality, the immediacy of this language bears some resemblance to the one Antonin Artaud postulates for the metaphysical act of acting that, for him, *is* the theatrical performance. On the spectator's side, this same immediacy provokes a reaction comparable to the one Artaud intends to achieve during the metaphysical act of watching that, for him, *is* the theatrical experience: laughter in its 'purest' form, that is anarchic laughter.

2.2. The answer to fate as expressed in physical and verbal language

The more man loses power over the environment they live in, the more human intentions grow meaningless, ultimately leading to the individual's losing their freedom of choice as well as of action. The human being becomes a plaything in the hands of fate while existence turns into a question of resigning to or defying the hostile conditions man is faced with. Comparing Buster Keaton to modern European theatre reveals one major difference in the portrayal of characters. Keaton's hero always retains his optimism even when confronted with the most dire situations, allowing him to assign them a certain meaning and, therefore, to uphold his confidence in his being able to defy them. The characters in the Theatre of the Absurd, by contrast, have become resigned to the fact that the world and, as a consequence, all life is meaningless.[98]

When Keaton's protagonist is forced to adapt his physical bearing to the – mostly mechanized – surroundings in order to overcome adverse circumstances, the naturalness of his human movements disappears, paradoxically, in a natural way. This reflects what Henri Bergson describes as '[…] une certaine *raideur de mécanique* là où l'on voudrait trouver la souplesse attentive et la flexibilité d'une personne'[99]. There are two scenes from Keaton's film *The General*, in particular, that illustrate this mechanization of human movement. The first one shows Keaton's character in the foreground chopping wood on the travelling locomotive. His movements are perfectly adapted to the demands and the rhythm of the machinery. Behind him in the background, a collective body of soldiers marching in the opposite direction forms a machinery of its own. It is a striking visual composition of one image capturing three mechanized processes simultaneously moving in three different directions. In another scene, the hero is seen riding on a wagon that is travelling on the railway tracks. Using all his force, he pushes the wagon's hand lever up and down in order to keep the vehicle running. His repetitive movements have, in fact, become the '[…] *mécanique plaquée sur du vivant* […]'[100], making Keaton's character the vehicle's engine. Bergson argues that the mechanical movement of a human being provokes the spectator's laughter because a mechanical movement is, by its very nature, repetitive not only in itself but also as an action.[101] Perhaps the most radical example illustrating Bergson's theory is Charlie Chaplin's film *Modern Times* (1936) where the comic hero is literally absorbed by his mechanized surroundings. While Keaton's protagonist assigns his repetitive movements a particular meaning and always employs them with a specific goal in mind, with Chaplin these movements have taken complete control of his hero's human nature and become mere ends in themselves.

The motif of – meaningless – repetition figures prominently also in twentieth-century European drama, and especially so in the plays of Eugène Ionesco and Samuel Beckett. In Ionesco's works, the characters start to lose their human nature, instead adopting the automatized nature of machines. This is reflected first and foremost in the playwright's use of language. *La Cantatrice Chauve* (1950) and *La Leçon* (1951)[102] are the most illustrative examples. In *La Leçon,* the disappearance of their human traits not only makes the characters appear ridiculous, but even leads to tragedy. In *La Cantatrice Chauve*, which Ionesco himself defines as 'anti-pièce' ('anti-play'), the characters find themselves in a situation that has no sense at all and that, at the end, becomes outright pathetic when all of them chorus in a loop: 'C'est pas par là, c'est par ici […]'[103]. Beckett's plays, for their part, convey an atmosphere that is rather somber but not entirely without tragicomic touches. Every now and then and as if on cue, his characters repeat specific actions and sentences. These repetitions reflect quiet despair and resignation on the part of the protagonists in the face of circumstances they will never be able to change. Their occasional and futile attempts to establish some coherence in their behaviour and speech symbolize a search for meaning in their existence, a search that leads nowhere. Whereas Keaton's heroes always expect their actions to result in a happy outcome, Beckett's Clov in *Fin de Partie,* for example, has climbed the ladder up and down countless times in his life without really knowing why. Even his hope – or fear – of finally seeing someone 'out there' vanishes into thin air. Announcements like 'Je te quitte' ('I leave you') are repeated again and again without carrying any meaning or bearing any consequence whatsoever. Both Ionesco's and Beckett's dramas paint a bleak picture of man in the modern world – a picture that is comic and tragic alike, thus underlining Ionesco's view that '[…] le comique est tragique, et la tragédie de l'homme, dérisoire'[104].

In using the aesthetic device of repetition, Buster Keaton and the playwrights of the Theatre of the Absurd draw on an element crucial to farce and vaudeville. In Keaton's films, the repetitious actions of a character always originate from an imperative necessity and enable the hero to defy adverse circumstances. With Ionesco and Beckett, by contrast, repetition is a compulsory part of the protagonists' speech and behaviour and does not fulfil any purpose. In a larger sense, then, it represents an ontological and universal emptiness. While Keaton's comic heroes in the end manage to shape their own destiny, the fate of the tragicomic protagonists of the Theatre of the Absurd is sealed from the beginning by an unknown and unseen force.

If a character's response to fate can express itself in extreme forms of motion, it can equally manifest itself in minimalism, that is in minute gestures and facial expressions or even complete stillness. In Keaton's films, the world surrounding the comic hero is always moving, visualized through crowds of people, wild chases, racing cars and trains, or storms and flooding. While Keaton usually makes his character react to the respective situation in typical vaudeville manner, he never allows his face to reveal any emotion. His 'frozen face', 'stone face' or 'dead pan', always displaying 'mute majesty'[105], contrasts sharply with his moving body. It is this juxtaposition of stillness and motion in Keaton's physical performance that contributes to the comic effect. At times, though, Keaton shows his character remaining physically calm, with his entire body freezing in place while being surrounded by turmoil. In the storm scene in *Steamboat Bill, Jr.*, houses and trees, cars and people are being carried away by violent gusts. Completely unaware that the front wall of a building is falling down on him, the comic hero stands motionless exactly on the spot where a windowless window frame hits the ground. Keaton's physical stillness reflects his character's momentary state of passiveness, of just being. The scene's absurd and almost surreal touches as well as its humour originate from and lie in the discrepancy between the stillness of a vulnerable human being and the motion of an environment out of control. In choosing this particular form of physical performance, Keaton once more emphasizes his character's confidence in fate and in his ability to defy even the worst dangers.

It is the mere presence of a character Alain Robbe-Grillet refers to when explaining that in Samuel Beckett's plays, more than in any other kind of theatre, the character simply is there, onstage. He goes on to argue that the nature of these plays does not allow the actor to act, it forces them to be.[106] Yet, it would be wrong to conclude that an actor's immobility means they do 'not act'. The acting shows in their facial play and their voice. In Beckett's *Happy Days*, the actress portraying Winnie has hardly any room to move, being buried to the waist in a low mound. Her gestures, laid down by Beckett in minute detail in his stage directions, are supposed to '"[…] follow the principle of grace and economy [...]"'[107]. With her facial play being equally economic, it is her eyes that are the most important means of expression as they alone convey the short moments of nostalgia and happiness she enjoys. While Winnie is still able to share memories with a fellow human being, Willie, and to experience emotions, the character of Krapp in Beckett's *Krapp's Last Tape* is cut off from any human contact, engaging only with a tape-recorder. Being confronted with his own self, his gaze betrays he is '"[…] trying to escape from himself [...]"'[108]. The extremely limited range of movements available to Beckett's protagonists mirrors and responds to the absence of a meaningful environment they could interact with.

Both in Keaton's films and Beckett's plays, minimalist gestures, minute facial expressions and complete physical immobility play a vital role in visualizing the relationship a character has with their own inner self and the world surrounding them. Most of all, though, they have become part of the storyline and, as such, have to be enacted so as to help develop and advance the plot. Referring to Buster Keaton, Clyde Bruckman put it succinctly: '"He showed them all how to underact. He could tell his story by lifting an eyebrow. He could tell his story by *not* lifting an eyebrow."'[109] In this respect, Beckett's theatre brings Keaton's art of silent film full circle.

The tragicomic condition of modern man as revealed through aesthetic multiplicity

'[…] Dreams, like the movies of the greatest silent comedians, are like humour stripped from its formulas and restraints, but at their best and deepest they are not funny.'[110]

On the face of it, this critic's view does not seem to apply to the silent film comedies of Buster Keaton. With him having always remained true to techniques practiced in *commedia dell'arte*, farce and vaudeville, his visual presentations of characters and events may appear as purely comic. Yet, Keaton combined these ancient aesthetic devices with the means film as an entirely new medium offered to couch serious issues such as social differences, the impact of technological development on the individual, and the condition of man in the modern world. It is, therefore, no exaggeration to consider Buster Keaton a link between old and new forms of aesthetic concepts and representation as well as between old and new aesthetics of humour. Although drawing on the grotesque, a crucial element of farce and especially vaudeville, he always grounded his characters and his films' dramatic starting point in reality. The stunts and slapstick he performed mostly served the storyline and thus were more than merely comic or ends in themselves. By making his physical performance part of the plot, he brought his comic's underlying grotesque nature closer to an implicitly serious reality and vice versa – as happens in (bad) dreams.

In the plays of twentieth-century European theatre, dramatic reality in all its seriousness increasingly grew grotesque itself, up to the point where the serious and the grotesque were no longer separable. This process went hand in hand with the playwrights' inventing and experimenting with new dramatic concepts that became ever more radical. The multiplicity of these concepts was accompanied by a multiplicity of aesthetic devices that ultimately knew no boundaries, with the language of performance reflecting the somber condition of modern man as shaped by the historical experiences of the twentieth century. Brecht and Pirandello employed various forms of meta-theatrical structure and language to display the bitter comic underlying their plays' serious dramatic realities. In the Theatre of the Absurd, it was dialogue and the language of – physical – performance, becoming increasingly illogical and grotesque, that illustrated the characters' tragicomic conditions. Artaud, the most radical of the theorists and playwrights discussed in this study, intended the language of performance to acquire a transcendental dimension.

In exploring and crossing artistic boundaries the way he did, Buster Keaton created a unique form of performance and representation. Being an American filmmaker trained on the vaudeville stage, he did not exactly seem to be the artist designated for anticipating the rich diversity of dramatic and aesthetic developments that would come to flourish on the stages of twentieth-century European theatre. Yet, this analysis has shown that Keaton and modern European playwrights did indeed share many approaches to artistic representation, both thematically and aesthetically. It is no coincidence, then, that it was precisely Buster Keaton who first brought to life onscreen an ideal formulated later by Eugène Ionesco for the stage, making the '[t]ragique et farce, prosaïsme et poétique, réalisme et fantastique, quotidien et insolite [...]'[111] coexist alongside each other. It found its expression in the aesthetic elegance of his silent film comedies.

Notes

[1]Anonymous critic, in *The New York Times*, in Walter Kerr, *The Silent Clowns*, New York: Da Capo Press, 1980: p.135.

[2]It is essential to point out that, due to their different origins, American and European vaudeville, with the latter being born in France, are of an entirely different nature. Whereas French vaudeville developped in the first half of the fifteenth century out of songs with a satirical and often malicious character and turned into two-act comedies (see Manfred Naumann (ed.), *Lexikon der französischen Literatur*, Leipzig: VEB Bibiliographisches Institut, 1987: pp.445-446), American vaudeville '[...] was [...] a kind of stream of consciousness of the theatre [where] [e]verything was thrown together [...]: ragtime and romantic ballad; grand opera and barbershop quartet; slapstick and Shakespeare; tap dancing and ballet; legerdemain and mental telepathy; juggling, tumbling, wire walking, aerial acrobats' (Rudi Blesh, *Keaton*, London: Secker & Warburg, 1967: p.39).

[3]The chapter on Luigi Pirandello's novel *Si gira!* (*Shoot!*) in *Pirandello and Film* by Nina da Vinci Nichols and Jana O'Keefe Bazzoni (Lincoln and London: University of Nebraska Press, 1995: pp.3-18) gives a detailed account of Pirandello's concerns with and contributions to film. Part II of the book presents documents by Pirandello such as a scenario and aesthetic treatises on cinema.

[4]It is important in this context to distinguish the terms *Verfremdung* and *Entfremdung*, which in early studies were usuallly both translated as 'alienation', although the first term rather means 'disillusion'. Only later did 'distanciation' and 'alienation' become the common translations of the term *Verfremdung*. Brecht uses *Entfremdung* closely in relation to Georg Wilhelm Friedrich Hegel and Karl Marx, yet in the sense of *Verfremdung*. Whereas for Hegel *Entfremdung* lies in the imaginative invention's becoming a materialistic product, Marx refers to it as to a – nearly hostile – distance of the human being to the product and to other human beings (see Werner Hecht et al. (eds.), 'Kommentar' in *Bertolt Brecht: Werke XXII: Schriften 2 (1933-1942) – Teil 2*, Berlin/Weimar: Aufbau Verlag; Frankfurt am Main: Suhrkamp Verlag, 1993: p.968 and pp. 969-970).

[5]Buster Keaton and Charles Samuels, *My Wonderful World of Slapstick*, New York: Da Capo Press, 1982: p.93.

[6]Robert Knopf, *The Theater and Cinema of Buster Keaton*, Princeton: Princeton University Press, 1999: pp.76-111.

[7]This is an abridged and paraphrased version of Manuela Gieri's comparison between Brecht and Pirandello. For the entire analysis see Manuela Gieri, 'Pirandello and the Theory of the Cinema', in *Contemporary Italian Filmmaking: Strategies of Subversion – Pirandello, Fellini, Scola, and the Directors of the New Generation*, Toronto, Buffalo, and London: University of Toronto Press, 1995: pp.30-81.

[8]Luigi Pirandello, *L'Umorismo*, ed. Luigi Battistelli, 2nd ed., Firenze: Saggio, 1920.
[Luigi Pirandello, *On Humour*, trans. Antonio Illiano and Daniel P. Testa, ed. Eugene H. Falk, Chapel Hill: University of North Carolina Press, 1974.]

[9]Pirandello, 1920: p.178.
'[t]he comic consists precisely of this *perception of the opposite*' [Pirandello, trans. A. Illiano and D.P. Testa, 1974: p.113].

[10]Pirandello, 1920: pp.178-179.
'[...] beyond, or rather [...] deeper into, the initial stage of awareness: from the beginning *perception of the opposite*, [it] has made me shift to a *feeling of the opposite*' [Pirandello, trans. A. Illiano and D.P. Testa, 1974: p.113].

[11]Pirandello, 1920: p.178.
'[...] detaching itself from it, analyzes it and disassembles its imagery [...]' [Pirandello, trans. A. Illiano and D.P. Testa, 1974: p.113].

[12]Bertolt Brecht, 'Episches Theater, Entfremdung', in *Bertolt Brecht: Werke XXII: Schriften 2 (1933-1942) – Teil 1*, eds. Werner Hecht et al., Berlin/Weimar: Aufbau Verlag; Frankfurt am Main: Suhrkamp Verlag, 1993: p.211.
The editors are not sure if it was indeed in 1936/1937 that Brecht wrote this essay.
'presenting things which appear natural as artificial' [translation by the author].

[13]Walter Benjamin, 'Was ist das epische Theater? [Erste Fassung]', in *Versuche über Brecht*, ed. Rolf Tiedemann, Frankfurt am Main: Suhrkamp Verlag, 1966: p.8.
[For the translation of the entire chapter see Walter Benjamin, 'What is Epic Theatre? [First Version]', in *Understanding Brecht*, trans. Anna Bostock, London and New York: Verso, 1998: pp.1-13.]

[14]Knopf, 1999, p.32.

[15]Knopf, 1999: p.50.

[16]Kerr, 1980: p.129.

[17]A profound analysis will follow in Chapter II.

[18]Luigi Pirandello, *Sei Personaggi in Cerca d'Autore* in 'Maschere Nude I', in *Opere di Luigi Pirandello*, vol.4, 3rd ed., Verona: Arnoldo Mondadori, 1965: pp.49-138.
[Luigi Pirandello, *Six Characters in Search of an Author*, in *Naked Masks: Five Plays by Luigi Pirandello*, trans. Edward Storer, ed. Eric Bentley, New York: E.P. Dutton, 1952: pp.209-276.]

[19]Luigi Pirandello, *Ciascuno a suo Modo*, in 'Maschere Nude I', in *Opere di Luigi Pirandello*, vol.4, 3rd ed., Verona: Arnoldo Mondadori, 1965: pp.139-220.
[Luigi Pirandello, *Each in his Own Way*, in *Naked Masks: Five Plays by Luigi Pirandello*, trans. Arthur Livingston, ed. Eric Bentley, New York: E.P. Dutton, 1952: pp.277-361.]

[20]Bertolt Brecht, 'Das Zeigen muss gezeigt werden', in *Bertolt Brecht: Werke XV: Gedichte 5 (1940-1956)*, eds. Werner Hecht et al., Berlin/Weimar: Aufbau Verlag; Frankfurt am Main: Suhrkamp Verlag, 1993: p.166.
[Berolt Brecht, 'Showing has to be shown', in *Bertolt Brecht: Poems 1913-1956*, trans. John Willett, eds. John Willett and Ralph Manheim, London: Methuen, 1976: pp:341-342.]

[21]Bertolt Brecht, in Julian H. Wulbern, *Brecht and Ionesco: Commitment and Context*, Urbana, Chicago, and London: University of Illinois Press, 1971: p.71.

[22]Pirandello, 1965: p.77.
'*The Father* […]. As a matter of fact … we have come here in search of an author …' [Pirandello, trans. E. Storer, 1952: p.215].

[23]Pirandello, 1965: p.218.
'*Signora Moreno*. She mimicked my voice! She used my manner – all my gestures! She was imitating me! I recognized myself!' [Pirandello, trans. A. Livingston, 1952: p.359.]

[24]Walter Denjamin, 'Das Kunstwerk im Zeitalter seiner technischen Reproduzierbarkeit', in *Illuminationen: Ausgewählte Schriften I*, Frankfurt am Main: Suhrkamp Verlag, 1977: pp.136-169.
[Walter Benjamin, 'The Work of Art in the Age of Mechanical Reproduction', in *Illuminations*, trans. Harry Zohn, ed. Hannah Arendt, London: Fontana Press, 1992: pp.211-244.]

[25]Benjamin, 1977: p.142.
[Benjamin, trans. H. Zohn, 1992: pp.216-217.]

[26]Benjamin, 1977: pp.152-153.
'The stage actor identifies himself with the character of his role. The film actor very often is denied this opportunity' [Benjamin, trans. H. Zohn, 1992: p.223].

27Benjamin, 1977: pp.152-153.
[Benjamin, trans. H.Zohn, 1992: p.223.]

28See note 11.

29Charles Baudelaire, 'De l'Essence du Rire et généralement du Comique dans les Arts Plastiques', in Œuvres Complètes de Charles Baudelaire, ed. Louis Conrad, Paris: MCMXXIII, 1923: p.396.
'[…] the existence […] of a permanent dualism, the capacity of being both himself and someone else at one and the same time' [Charles Baudelaire, 'Of the Essence of Laughter, and generally of the Comic in the Plastic Arts', in Baudelaire: Selected Writings on Art and Literature, trans. P.E. Charvet, London: Penguin Books, 1992: p.160].

30Clyde Bruckman, in Blesh, 1967: pp.146-152.

31Keaton and Samuels, 1982: pp.134-135.

32Keaton and Samuels, 1982: pp.173-176.

33Henry Jenkins, in Knopf, 1999: p.39.

34Keaton, in Blesh, 1967: p.142.

35da Vinci Nichols and O'Keefe Bazzoni, 1995: p.35.

36Samuel Beckett, Warten auf Godot/En attendant Godot/Waiting for Godot, trans. Elmar Tophoven, Frankfurt am Main: Suhrkamp Verlag, 1971.

37This gag is a parody of the real conditions in Hollywood at the time when Thomas H. Ince appeared on each film credit as the man in charge of everything. Keaton explained his idea in the following way: 'I don't deserve any credit […] Thomas H. Ince was my ince-spiration.' (Keaton, in Blesh, 1967: p.167).

38Pirandello, 1965: p.143.
'[…] it appears that Pirandello has taken the subject of his new comedy Each in his Own Way, which is going to be represented at the theatre … tonight, from the extremely dramatic suicide of the mourned young sculptor Giacomo la Vela, which occurred a few months ago in Turin' [translation by the author].

39See 'Primo Intermezzo Corale', in Pirandello, 1965: pp.177-186.
['First Choral Interlude', in Pirandello, trans. A. Livingston, 1952: pp.311-325.]

40Benjamin, 1977: p.152.
[see Benjamin, trans. H. Zohn, 1992: p.223.]

41Pirandello, in Gieri, 1995: pp.53-54.
'"[…] not only from the stage, but also in a sense from themselves. Because their action, the live action of their live bodies, there, on the screen of the cinematograph no longer exists: it is their image alone, caught in a moment, in a gesture, in an expression, that flickers and disappears"' [Pirandello, trans. M. Gieri, in Gieri, 1995: pp.53-54].

42Pirandello, in Gieri, 1995: p.54.
[Pirandello, trans. M. Gieri, in Gieri, 1995: p.54.]

43See Bertolt Brecht, 'Gegensatz des Schauspielers zur Figur', in Bertolt Brecht: Werke XXII: Schriften 2 (1933-1942) – Teil 1, eds. Werner Hecht et al., Berlin/Weimar: Aufbau Verlag; Frankfurt am Main: Suhrkamp Verlag, 1993: pp.221-222.

44Brecht, in Benjamin, 1966: p.18.
'"The actor must show an event, and he must show himself. He naturally shows the event by showing himself, and he shows himself by showing the event. Although these two tasks coincide, they must not coincide to such

a point that the contrast (difference) between them disappears"' [Brecht, in Benjamin, trans. A. Bostock, 1998: p.11].

[45]For the entire text see Bertolt Brecht, 'Die Straßenszene', in *Bertolt Brecht:Werke XXII: Schriften 2 (1933-1942) – Teil 1*, eds. Werner Hecht et al., Berlin/Weimar: Aufbau Verlag; Frankfurt am Main: Suhrkamp Verlag, 1993: pp.370-381.

[46]Brecht, in Walter Benjamin, 'Was ist das epische Theater? [Zweite Fassung]', in Benjamin, 1966: p.27.
'"[m]aking gestures quotable"' [Brecht, in Benjamin, 'What is Epic Theatre? [Second Version]', in Benjamin, trans. A. Bostock, 1998: p.19].

[47]Benjamin, 1966: p.27.
'[…] the more often we interrupt someone in process of action […]' [Benjamin, trans. A. Bostock, 1998: p.20].

[48]Samuel Beckett, *Film*, in *Samuel Beckett: The Complete Dramatic Works*, London and Boston: Faber and Faber, 1990: pp.321-334.

[49]Henri Bergson, 'Le Rire: Essai sur la Signification du Comique', in *Henri Bergson: Œuvres*, ed. André Robinet, 2nd ed., Paris: Presses Universitaires de France, 1963: p.453.
[For the translation of the entire essay see Henri Bergson, 'Laughter', in *Comedy*, translator unknown, ed. Wylie Sypher, Baltimore and London: John Hopkins University Press, 1983: pp.61-190.]

[50]Pirandello, 1920: p.172.
'[…] a fundamental "contradiction" which is usually said to derive principally from the discord which feeling and meditation discover either between real life and the human ideal or between human aspirations and human frailty and miseries […]' [Pirandello, trans. A. Illiano and D.P. Testa, 1974: p.109].

[51]Gerald Mast, *The Comic Mind: Comedy and the Movies*, 2nd ed., Chicago and London: University of Chicago Press, 1979: p.20.

[52]Mast, 1979: p.129.

[53]Herbert Read, 'Rational Society and Irrational Art', in *Art and Alienation: The Role of the Artist in Society*, London: James and Hudson, 1967: p.37.

[54]Bertolt Brecht, *Mann ist Mann*, in *Bertolt Brecht: Werke II: Stücke 2*, eds. Werner Hecht et al., Berlin/Weimar: Aufbau-Verlag; Frankfurt am Main: Suhrkamp Verlag, 1988: pp.93-227.
[Bertolt Brecht, *Man Equals Man*, in *Bertolt Brecht: Collected Plays*, vol.2i, trans. Gerhard Nellhaus, eds. John Willett and Ralph Manheim, London: Eyre Methuen, 1979: pp.1-76.]

[55]Brecht, 1988: pp.202-203.
'Herr Bertolt Brecht maintains man equals man
[…]
But then Herr Brecht points out how far one can
Manoeuvre and manipulate that man.
[…]
He has some kind friends by whom he is pressed
Entirely in his own interest
To conform with this world and its twists and turns
And give up pursuing his own fishy concerns.
[…]' [Brecht, trans. G. Nellhaus, 1979: p.38.]

[56]Terry Hodgson, *Modern Drama: From Ibsen to Fugard*, London: B.T. Batsford, 1992: p.38.

[57]Bertolt Brecht, *Mutter Courage und ihre Kinder*, in *Bertolt Brecht: Werke VI: Stücke 6*, eds. Werner Hecht et al., Berlin/Weimar: Aufbau-Verlag; Frankfurt am Main: Suhrkamp Verlag, 1989: pp.7-86.
[Bertolt Brecht, *Mother Courage and her Children*, trans. John Willett, London: Methuen, 1983.]

[58]Robert Abirached, *La Crise du Personnage dans le Théâtre Moderne*, Paris: Éditions Grasset & Fasquelle, 1978: p.287.
'[…] to establish a compromise between the reasonable and the irrational […]' [translation by the author].

[59]Gieri, 1995: p.67.

[60]Knopf, 1999: p.21.

[61]Bertolt Brecht, in Brian Doherty (ed.), *Twentieth-Century European Drama*, London: Macmillan Press, 1994: p.28.

[62]Nevertheless, self-alienation has become a serious social and political issue since the industrial revolution. Karl Marx explains in his essay "[Die entfremdete Arbeit]" in his 'Ökonomisch-phlosophische Manuskripte aus dem Jahre 1844 [Auszug]' in detail in what way the human being is alienated from themselves as well as from the objects they produce and from their fellow human beings, as the process of working and producing, comparable to the condition of slavery, deprives them of any closeness to material and humanity (see *Karl Marx/Friedrich Engels: Ausgewählte Werke in sechs Bänden*, vol.I, 8th ed., eds. Richard Sperl and Hanni Wettengel, Berlin: Dietz Verlag, 1979: pp.82-96).

[63]Bergson, 1963: p.401.
'[…] *that body reminds us of a mere machine* […]' [Bergson, trans. unknown, 1983: p.79].

[64]This film was a reaction to trials and public condemnation of his friend and colleague Roscoe Arbuckle because of alleged murder [See Blesh, 1967: pp.198-203].

[65]Eugène Ionesco, *Jacques ou La Soumission*, in *Eugène Ionesco: Théâtre Complet*, ed. Emmanuel Jacquart, Paris: Éditions Gallimard, 1981: pp.85-113.
[Eugène Ionesco, *Jacques or Obedience*, in *Eugène Ionesco: Plays*, vol.1, trans. Donald Watson, London: John Calder, 1961: pp.121-150.]

[66]See Buster Keaton, 'Quand la Comédie est Chose Sérieuse' (1928), in, *Cahiers du Cinéma*, No. 296, January 1979: pp.21-22.

[67]Blesh, 1967: p.199.

[68]Walter Kerr, *Tragedy and Comedy*, New York: Simon and Schuster, 1967: p.210.

[69]Brecht, 1988: p.226.
'*The soldiers bring in the things and make a ring round Galy Gay so as to hide him from the audience. Meanwhile the band plays the war march […].*
The ring of soldiers opens […] Galy Gay in the middle bristling with assorted weapons […].'
[Brecht, trans. G. Nellhaus, 1979: p.133; as there does not exist an English translation of the play's second version, the editors of the existent English version have included this additional scene in their 'Editorial Notes'.]

[70]Ionesco, 1981: p.93.
'Jacques *[like an automaton]*
"I love potatoes in their jackets!
I love potatoes in their jackets!
I love potatoes in their jackets!"'
[Ionesco, trans. D. Watson, 1961: p.128.]

[71]Ionesco, 1981: p.94.
'The Mother: "Gaston, if that's how things are, in that case we can marry him off […]"' [Ionesco, trans. D. Watson, 1961: p.130].

[72]Erich Franzen, *Formen des modernen Dramas: Von der Illusionsbühne zum Anti-Theater*, München: Verlag C.H.

Beck, 1970: p.59.

[73]Karl S. Guthke, *Die Moderne Tragikomödie: Theorie und Gestalt*, trans. Gerhard Raabe and Karl S. Guthke, Göttingen: Vandenhoeck & Ruprecht, 1968: p.45.

[74]Guthke, trans. G. Raabe and K.S. Guthke, 1968: pp.90-91 and pp.109-110.

[75]Keaton, 1982: pp.11-83.

[76]Keaton, 1982: p.13.

[77]Knopf, 1999: pp.37-38.

[78]Antonin Artaud, 'La mise en scène et la métaphysique', in *Le Théâtre et son Double*, Paris: Éditions Gallimard, 1964: p.55.
'[…] a tangible, physical place that needs to be filled and it ought to be allowed to speak its own concrete language' [Antonin Artaud, 'Production and Metaphysics', in *The Theatre and its Double*, trans. Victor Corti, London: John Calder, 1985: p.27].

[79]Artaud, 1964: p.56.
[Artaud, trans. V. Corti, 1985: p.27.]

[80]Artaud, 1964: pp. 57-58.
For the entire chapter see Artaud, 1964: pp.49-71 [Artaud, trans. V. Corti, 1985: pp.23-33].

[81]Bergson, 1963: p.410.
'[…] any substitution whatsoever of the artificial for the natural' [Bergson, translator unknown, 1983: p.91].

[82]Antonin Artaud, 'Le Théâtre de la Cruauté', in Artaud, 1964: p.152.
'[t]he actor is both a prime factor, since the show's success depends on the effectiveness of his acting, as well as a kind of neutral, pliant factor since he is rigorously denied any individual initiative' [Antonin Artaud, 'The Theatre of Cruelty', in Artaud, trans. V. Corti, 1985: p.76].

[83]Bruckman, in Blesh, 1967: p.252.

[84]Kevin Brownlow and David Gill (wr. and dir.), *Buster Keaton – A Hard Act to Follow*, Thames Television, 1987.

[85]Artaud, 1964: p.64.
[Artaud, trans. V. Corti, 1985: pp.31-32.]

[86]Abirached, 1978: p.359.

[87]Eugène Ionesco, *Notes et Contre-Notes*, Paris: Éditions Gallimard, 1962: p.32.

[88]Ionesco, 1962: p.16.
'It is not only allowed but advisable to make props play, to make objects live, to animate the scenery, to represent symbols in a concrete way. Just as the word is continued in gesture, in play and in pantomime, which, as soon as the word proves to be insufficient, replace the word, the material stage elements can extend the word' [translation by the author].

[89]Keaton, 1982: p.142.

[90]Knopf, 1999: p.75.

[91]Martin Esslin, 'Introduction', in *The Theatre of the Absurd*, 3rd ed., Hammondsworth: Penguin Books, 1983: p.23.

[92]Samuel Beckett, *Fin de Partie*, Paris: Éditions de Minuit, 1957: p.25.

'Nature has forgotten us.'
'There's no more nature.'
[Samuel Beckett, *Endgame*, in *Samuel Beckett: The Complete Dramatic Works*, London and Boston: Faber and Faber, 1990: p.97]

[93]Knopf, 1999: p.75.

[94]George E. Wellwarth, *Modern Drama and the Death of God*, Wisconsin: University of Wisconsin Press, 1986: p.47.

[95]Artaud, 1964: p.63.
'Current theatre is in decline because on the one hand it has lost any feeling for seriousness, and on the other for laughter. Because it has broken away from solemnity, from direct, harmful effectiveness – in a word from Danger.
For it has lost any true sense of humour, and laughter's physical, anarchic, dissolving power' [Artaud, trans. V. Corti, 1985: p.31].

[96]Christine Olga Kiebuzinska, in Gene A. Plunka, (ed.), *Antonin Artaud and the Modern Theatre*, Rutherford, Madison, and Teaneck: Fairleigh Dickinson University Press; London and Toronto: Associated University Presses, 1994: p.149.

[97]For the entire chapter see Artaud, 1964: pp.49-71 [Artaud, trans. V. Corti, 1985: pp.23-33].

[98]It is important to distinguish the thematic and aesthetic concept of the Theatre of the Abusrd from that of the Theatre of Existentialism: the first abandons any rational thinking to analyze the senselessness of being; the second still displays logical reasoning in its approach to irrationality. (For a detailed distinction between the two dramatic and philosophical concepts see Esslin, 1983: pp.19-28.)

[99]Bergson, 1963: p.391.
'[…] a certain *mechanical inelasticity*, just where one would expect to find the wide-awake adaptability and the living pliableness of a human being' [Bergson, translator unknown, 1983: p.67].

[100] Bergson, 1963: p.405.
'[…] *mechanical encrusted on the living* […]' [Bergson, translator unknown, 1983: p.84].

[101]See Bergson, 1963: pp.429-431.
[See Bergson, translator unknown, 1983: pp.119-121.]

[102]Eugène Ionesco, *La Leçon*, in *Eugène Ionesco: Théâtre Complet*, ed. Emmanuel Jacquart, Paris: Éditions Gallimard, 1981: pp.43-75.
[Eugène Ionesco, *The Lesson*, in *Eugène Ionesco: Plays*, vol.1, trans. Donald Watson, London: John Calder, 1961: pp.3-37.]

[103]Eugène Ionesco, *La Cantatrice Chauve*, in *Eugène Ionesco: Théâtre Complet*, ed. Emmanuel Jacquart, Paris: Éditions Gallimard, 1981: p.42.
'It's not that way, it's this way […]' [Eugène Ionesco, *The Bald Primadonna*, in *Eugène Ionesco: Plays*, vol.1, trans. Donald Watson, London: John Calder, 1961: p.119].

[104]Ionesco, 1962: p.14.
'[…] the comic is tragic, and the tragic of man is pathetic' [translation by the author].

[105]See Kerr, 1980: p.217.

[106]Alain Robbe-Grillet, 'Retour à la Signification', in *Les Critiques de Notre Temps et Beckett*, ed. Dominique Nores, Paris: Éditions Garnier Frères, 1971: pp.142-150.
[Alain Robbe-Grillet, 'Samuel Beckett, or "Presence' in the Theatre"', in *Samuel Beckett: A Collection of Critical Essays*, ed. Martin Esslin, Englewood Cliffs: Prentice Hall, 1965: pp.108-116.]

[107]Samuel Beckett, *The Theatrical Notebooks of Samuel Beckett: 'Happy Days: The Production Notebook of Samuel Beckett'*, ed. James Knowlson, London and Boston: Faber and Faber, 1985: p.159, note 2.

[108]Samuel Beckett, in *The Theatrical Notebooks of Samuel Beckett: 'Volume III: Krapp's Last Tape'*, ed. James Knowlson, London: Faber and Faber, 1992: p.23, note 78.

[109]Bruckman, in Blesh, 1967: p.149.

[110]Anonymous critic, in *The New York Times*, in Kerr, 1980: p.135.

[111]Ionesco, 1962: p.15.
    '[t]ragedy and farce, the prosaic and the poetic, realism and fantasy, the ordinary and the unusual [...]' [translation by the author].

Primary Sources

I. Films

1. Keaton Silent Shorts

One Week, Producer: Joseph M. Schenck; Director/Script: Buster Keaton and Eddie Cline; Metro
Pictures, 1920.

Cast: Buster Keaton, Sybil Seely, Joe Roberts.

The High Sign, Producer: Joseph M. Schenck; Director/Script: Buster Keaton and Eddie Cline;
Metro Pictures, 1921.

Cast: Buster Keaton, Bartine Burkett, Al St. John (cameo).

The Playhouse, Producer: Joseph M. Schenck; Director/Script: Buster Keaton and Eddie Cline;
First National, 1921.

Cast: Buster Keaton, Virginia Fox, Joe Roberts.

Cops, Producer: Joseph M. Schenck; Director/Script: Buster Keaton and Eddie Cline; First
National, 1922.

Cast: Buster Keaton, Virginia Fox, Joe Roberts, Eddie Cline.

Film, Producer: Barney Rosset; Director: Alan Schneider; Script: Samuel Beckett; An Evergreen
Theatre Production, 1965.

Cast: Buster Keaton, James Karen, Nell Harrison, Susan Reed.

2. Keaton Silent Features

The Three Ages, Producer: Joseph M. Schenck; Directors: Buster Keaton and Eddie Cline; Script:
Clyde Bruckman, Joseph Mitchell, and Jean Havez; Metro Pictures, 1923.

Cast: Buster Keaton, Margaret Leahy, Wallace Beery, Joe Roberts et al.

Our Hospitality, Producer: Joseph M. Schenck; Directors: Buster Keaton and Jack C. Blystone;
Script: Clyde Bruckman, Joseph Mitchell, and Jean Havez; Metro Pictures, 1923.

Cast: Buster Keaton, Buster Keaton, Jr., Kitty Bradbury, Joe Keaton, Natalie Talmadge et al.

Sherlock Jr., Producer: Joseph M. Schenck; Director: Buster Keaton; Script: Clyde Bruckman,
Joseph Mitchell, and Jean Havez; Metro Pictures, 1923.

Cast: Buster Keaton, Kathryn McGuire, Ward Crane, Joe Keaton et al.

The Navigator, Producer: Joseph M. Schenck; Directors: Buster Keaton and Donald Crisp; Script:
Clyde Bruckman, Joseph Mitchell, and Jean Havez; Metro-Goldwyn Pictures Corp., 1924.

Cast: Buster Keaton, Kathryn McGuire, Frederick Vroom et al.

The General, Producer: Joseph M. Schenck; Directors: Buster Keaton and Clyde Bruckman; Script: Buster Keaton and Clyde Bruckman; United Artists, 1927.

  Cast: Buster Keaton, Marion Mack, Charles Smith, Frank Barnes et al.

Steamboat Bill, Jr., Producer: Joseph M. Schenck; Director: Charles F. Reisner; Script: Carl Harbaugh; United Artists, 1928.

  Cast: Buster Keaton, Ernest Torrence, Tom Lewis, Tom McGuire et al.

The Cameraman, Producer: Lawrence Weingarten; Director: Edward M. Sedgwick; Script: Richard Schayer; MGM, 1928.

  Cast: Buster Keaton, Marceline Day, Harold Goodwin, Sidney Bracy, Josephine (monkey) et al.

3. Other Films

Intolerance, Producer/Director: D.W. Griffith; Script: D.W. Griffith et al.; Triangle Distributing Corporation, 1916.

  Cast: Lillian Gish, Mae Marsh, Howard Gaye, Erich von Stroheim et al.

Modern Times, Producer/ Director/ Script: Charles Chaplin; United Artists, 1936.

  Cast: Charles Chaplin, Paulette Goddard, Henry Bergman, Stanley J. Sanford et al.

II. Plays

Beckett, Samuel, *Warten auf Godot/En attendant Godot/Waiting for Godot*, trans. Elmar Tophoven, Frankfurt am Main: Suhrkamp Verlag, 1971.

Beckett, Samuel, *Fin de Partie*, Paris: Éditions de Minuit, 1957.

  – *Endgame*, in *Samuel Beckett: The Complete Dramatic Works*, London and Boston: Faber and Faber, 1990: pp.89-134.

Beckett, Samuel, *Happy Days*, in *Samuel Beckett: The Complete Dramatic Works*, London and Boston: Faber and Faber, 1990: pp.135-168.

Beckett, Samuel, *Krapp's Last Tape*, in *Samuel Beckett: The Complete Dramatic Works*, London and Boston: Faber and Faber, 1990: pp.213-223.

Brecht, Bertolt, *Mann ist Mann*, in *Bertolt Brecht: Werke II: Stücke 2*, eds. Werner Hecht et al., Berlin/Weimar: Aufbau-Verlag; Frankfurt am Main: Suhrkamp Verlag, 1988: pp.93-227.

  – *Man Equals Man*, in *Bertolt Brecht: Collected Plays*, vol.2i, trans. Gerhard Nellhaus, eds. John Willet and Ralph Manheim, London: Eyre Methuen, 1979: pp.1-76.

Brecht, Bertolt, *Mutter Courage und ihre Kinder*, in *Bertolt Brecht: Werke VI: Stücke 6*, eds. Werner Hecht et al., Berlin/Weimar: Aufbau-Verlag; Frankfurt am Main: Suhrkamp Verlag, 1989: pp.7-86.

–   *Mother Courage and her Children*, trans. John Willett, London: Methuen, 1983.

Ionesco, Eugène, *Jacques ou La Soumission*, in *Eugène Ionesco: Théâtre Complet*, ed. Emmanuel Jacquart, Paris: Éditions Gallimard, 1981: pp.85-113.

–   *Jacques or Obedience*, in *Eugène Ionesco: Plays*, vol.1, trans. Donald Watson, London: John Calder, 1961: pp.121-150.

Ionesco, Eugène, *La Cantatrice Chauve*, in *Eugène Ionesco: Théâtre Complet*, ed. Emmanuel Jacquart, Paris: Éditions Gallimard, 1981: pp.7-42.

–   *The Bald Primadonna*, in *Eugène Ionesco: Plays*, vol.1, trans. Donald Watson, London: John Calder, 1961: pp.85-119.

Ionesco, Eugène, *La Leçon*, in *Eugène Ionesco: Théâtre Complet*, ed. Emmanuel Jacquart, Paris: Éditions Gallimard, 1981: pp.43-75.

–   *The Lesson*, in *Eugène Ionesco: Plays*, vol.1, trans. Donald Watson, London: John Calder, 1961: pp.3-37.

Pirandello, Luigi, *Ciascuno a suo Modo*, in *Maschere Nude I*, in *Opere di Luigi Pirandello*, vol.4, 3rd ed., Verona: Arnoldo Mondadori, 1965: pp.139-220.

–   *Each in his Own Way*, in *Naked Masks: Five Plays by Luigi Pirandello*, trans. Arthur Livingston, ed. Eric Bentley, New York: E.P. Dutton, 1952: pp.277-361.

Pirandello, Luigi, *Sei Personaggi in Cerca d'Autore*, in *Maschere Nude I*, in *Opere di Luigi Pirandello*, vol.4, 3rd ed., Verona: Arnoldo Mondadori, 1965: pp.49-138.

–   *Six Characters in Search of an Author*, in *Naked Masks: Five Plays by Luigi Pirandello*, trans. Edward Storer, ed. Eric Bentley, New York: E.P. Dutton, 1952: pp.209-276.

III. Poem

Brecht, Bertolt, 'Das Zeigen muss gezeigt werden', in *Bertolt Brecht: Werke XV: Gedichte 5 (1940-1956)*, eds. Werner Hecht et al., Berlin/Weimar: Aufbau-Verlag; Frankfurt am Main: Suhrkamp Verlag, 1993: p.166.

–   'Showing has to be shown', in *Bertolt Brecht: Poems 1913-1956*, trans. John Willett, eds. John Willett and Ralph Manheim, London: Methuen, 1976: pp.341-342.

IV. The Theatrical Notebooks of Samuel Beckett

Beckett, Samuel, *The Theatrical Notebooks of Samuel Beckett: 'Volume III: Krapp's Last Tape'*, ed. James Knowlson, London: Faber and Faber, 1992.

Beckett, Samuel, *The Theatrical Notebooks of Samuel Beckett: 'Happy Days: The Production Notebook of Samuel Beckett'*, ed. James Knowslon, London and Boston: Faber and Faber, 1985.

V. Theoretical Writings

1. Books

Artaud, Antonin, *Le Théâtre et son Double*, Paris: Éditions Gallimard, 1964.

–   *The Theatre and its Double*, trans. Victor Corti, London: John Calder, 1985.

Benjamin, Walter, *Versuche über Brecht*, ed. Rolf Tiedemann, Frankfurt am Main: Suhrkamp Verlag, 1966.

–   *Understanding Brecht*, trans. Anna Bostock. London and New York: Verso, 1998.

Brecht, Bertolt, *Werke XXII: Schriften 2 (1933-1942) – Teil 1*, eds. Werner Hecht et al., Berlin/Weimar: Aufbau Verlag; Frankfurt am Main: Suhrkamp Verlag, 1993.

Brecht, Bertolt, *Werke XXII: Schriften 2 (1933-1942) – Teil 2*, eds. Werner Hecht et al., Berlin/Weimar: Aufbau Verlag; Frankfurt am Main: Suhrkamp Verlag, 1993.

Ionesco, Eugène, *Notes et Contre-Notes*, Paris: Éditions Gallimard, 1962.

Pirandello, Luigi, *L'Umorismo*, ed. Luigi Battistelli, 2nd ed., Firenze: Saggio, 1920.

–   *On Humour*, trans. Antonio Illiano and Daniel P. Testa, ed. Eugene H. Falk, Chapel Hill: University of North Carolina Press, 1974.

2. Essays

Baudelaire, Charles, 'De l'Essence du Rire et généralement du Comique dans les Arts Plastiques', in *Œuvres Complètes de Charles Baudelaire*, Paris: Éditions Louis Conrad, 1922: pp.369-396.

–   'Of the Essence of Laughter, and generally of the Comic in the Plastic Arts', in *Baudelaire: Selected Writings on Art and Literature*, trans. P.E. Charvet, London: Penguin Books, 1992: pp.140-161.

Benjamin, Walter, 'Das Kunstwerk im Zeitalter seiner technischen Reproduzierbarkeit', in *Illuminationen: Ausgewählte Schriften I*, Frankfurt am Main: Suhrkamp Verlag, 1977: pp.136-169.

–   'The Work of Art in the Age of Mechanical Reproduction', in *Illuminations*, trans. Harry Zohn, ed. Hannah Arendt, London: Fontana Press, 1992: pp.211-244.

Bergson, Henri, 'Le Rire: Essai sur la Signification du Comique', in *Henri Bergson: Œuvres*, ed. André Robinet, 2nd ed., Paris: Presses Universitaires de France, 1963: pp.387- 485.

–   'Laughter', in *Comedy*, no translator, ed. Wylie Sypher, Baltimore and London: John Hopkins University Press, 1983: pp.61-190.

Marx, Karl, "[Die entfremdete Arbeit]", in 'Ökonomisch-philosophische Manuskripte aus dem Jahre 1844 [Auszug]', in *Karl Marx/Friedrich Engels: Ausgewählte Werke in sechs Bänden*, vol.I, 8th ed., eds. Richard Sperl and Hanni Wettengel, Berlin: Dietz Verlag, 1979: pp.82-96.

Secondary Sources

I. On Buster Keaton

1. Books

Blesh, Rudi, *Keaton*, London: Secker & Warburg, 1967.

Keaton, Buster and Samuels, Charles, *My Wonderful World of Slapstick*, New York: Da Capo Press, 1982.

Knopf, Robert, *The Theater and Cinema of Buster Keaton*, Princeton: Princeton University Press, 1999.

2. Documentary

Buster Keaton – A Hard Act to Follow, wr. and dir. Kevin Brownlow and David Gill, Thames Television, 1987.

II. Secondary Sources

1. Books

Abirached, Robert, *La Crise du Personnage dans le Théâtre Moderne*, Paris: Éditions Grasset & Fasquelle, 1978.

Esslin, Martin, *The Theatre of the Absurd*, 3rd. ed., Hammondsworth: Penguin Books, 1983.

Franzen, Erich, *Formen des modernen Dramas: Von der Illusionsbühne zum Anti-Theater*, München: Verlag C.H. Beck, 1970.

Gieri, Manuela, *Contemporary Italian Filmmaking: Strategies of Subversion – Pirandello, Fellini, Scola, and the Directors of the New Generation*, Toronto, Buffalo, and London: University of Toronto Press, 1995.

Guthke, Karl S., *Die Moderne Tragikomödie: Theorie und Gestalt*, trans. Gerhard Raabe and Karl S. Guthke, Göttingen: Vandenhoeck & Ruprecht, 1968.

Hodgson, Terry, *Modern Drama: From Ibsen to Fugard*, London: B.T. Batsford, 1992.

Kerr, Walter, *The Silent Clowns*, New York: Da Capo Press, 1980.

Kerr, Walter, *Tragedy and Comedy*, New York: Simon and Schuster, 1967.

Mast, Gerald, *The Comic Mind: Comedy and the Movies*, 2nd ed., Chicago and London: University of Chicago Press, 1979.

Naumann, Manfred (ed.), *Lexikon der Französischen Literatur*, Leipzig: VEB Bibliographisches
    Institut, 1987.

da Vinci Nichols, Nina and O'Keefe Bazzoni, Jana, *Pirandello and Film*, Lincoln and London:
    University of Nebraska Press, 1995.

Plunka, Gene A. (ed.), *Antonin Artaud and the Modern Theatre*, Rutherford, Madison, and Teaneck:
    Fairleigh Dickinson University Press; London and Toronto: Associated University
    Presses, 1994.

Wellwarth, George E., *Modern Drama and the Death of God*, Wisconsin: University of Wisconsin
    Press, 1986.

Wulbern, Julian H., *Brecht and Ionesco: Commitment in Context*, Urbana, Chicago, and London:
    University of Illinois Press, 1971.

2. Essays

Read, Herbert, 'Rational Society and Irrational Art', in *Art and Alienation: The Role of the Artist in
    Society*, London: James and Hudson, 1967: pp.14-42.

Robbe-Grillet, Alain, 'Retour à la Signification', in *Les Critiques de Notre Temps et Beckett*, ed.
    Dominique Nores, Paris: Éditions Garnier Frères, 1971: pp.142-150.

–   'Samuel Beckett, or "Presence' in the Theatre"', in *Samuel Beckett: A Collection of
    Critical Essays*, ed. Martin Esslin, Englewood Cliffs: Prentice Hall, 1965: pp.108-
    116.

3. Article

Keaton, Buster, 'Quand la Comédie est Chose Sérieuse' (1928), in *Cahiers du Cinéma*, No.296,
    January 1997: pp.21-22.

Further Reading

I. On Buster Keaton

1. Books

Benayoun, Robert, *The Look of Buster Keaton*, ed. and trans. Randall Conrad, London: Pavilion Books, 1984.

Robinson, David, *Buster Keaton*, eds. Penelope Houston et al., 2nd ed., London: Thames & Hudson, in association with the BFI, 1970.

2. Documentary

The Golden Age of Buster Keaton, dir. Jay Ward, Jay Ward Prod. and Buster Keaton Prod., 1975.

II. The Theatrical Notebooks of Samuel Beckett

Beckett, Samuel, *Film*, in *Samuel Beckett: The Complete Dramatic Works*, London and Boston: Faber and Faber, 1990: pp.321-334.

Beckett, Samuel, *The Theatrical Notebooks of Samuel Beckett: 'Volume I: Waiting for Godot'*, eds. Dougald McMillan and James Knowlson, London: Faber and Faber, 1993.

Beckett, Samuel, *The Theatrical Notebooks of Samuel Beckett:'Volume II: Endgame'*, ed. S.E. Gontarski, London: Faber and Faber, 1992.

III. Secondary Sources

1. Books

Abel, Richard (ed.), *Silent Film*, London: Athlone Press, 1996.

Arnheim, Rudolf, *Film as Art*, London: Faber and Faber, 1958.

Arnheim, Rudolf, *Film Essays and Criticism*, trans. Brenda Benthien, Wisconsin: University of Wisconsin Press, 1997.

Balázs, Béla, *Theory of Film (Character and Growth of a New Art)*, trans. Edith Bone, New York: Arno Press and The New York Times, 1972.

Butler, Lance St. John, *Samuel Beckett and the Meaning of Being: A Study in Ontological Parable*, London: Macmillan Press, 1984.

Doherty, Brian (ed.), *Twentieth-Century European Drama*, Palgrave: Macmillan Press, 1994.

Duckworth, Colin, *Dramatic Effect in Samuel Beckett with a Special Reference to Eugène Ionesco*, London: George Allen and Unwin, 1972.

Elsaesser, Thomas and Barker, Adam (eds.), *Early Cinema: Space, Frame, Narrative*, London: BFI, 1990.

Fletcher, John (ed.), *Forces in Modern French Drama: Studies in Variations on the Permitted Lie*, London: University of London Press, 1972.

Gilbert, Douglas, *American Vaudeville: Its Life and Times*, New York: Dover Publications, 1963.

Hurt, James (ed.), *Focus on Film and Theatre*, Englewood Cliffs: Prentice Hall, 1973.

Jarry, Alfred, *Ansichten über das Theater*, trans. Brigitte Weidmann, Zürich: Verlags AG Die Arche, 1970.

Kleber, Pia and Visser, Colin (eds.), *Re-interpreting Brecht: His Influence on Contemporary Drama and Film*, Cambridge University Press, 1992.

Le Théâtre Moderne II: Depuis la Deuxième Guerre Mondiale, Paris: Éditions du Centre National de la Recherche Scientifique, 1967.

Nelson, T.G.A., *Comedy: An Introduction to Comedy in Literature, Drama and Cinema*, Oxford and New York: Oxford University Press, 1990.

Palmer, Jerry, *The Logic of the Absurd: On Film and Television Comedy*, London: BFI, 1987.

Robinson, David, *The Great Funnies: A History of Film Comedy*, London: Studio Vista, 1969.

Stein, Charles W. (ed.), *American Vaudeville as seen by its Contemporaries*, New York: Alfred A. Knopf, 1984.

Szondi, Peter, *Theorie des modernen Dramas*, Frankfurt am Main: Suhrkamp Verlag, 1964.

–   *Theory of the Modern Drama*, ed. and trans. Michael Hays, Cambridge: Polity Press, 1987.

2. Essays

Bryden, Mary, 'Solitude, Stillness, Silence and Stars', in *Samuel Beckett and the Idea of God*, New York and London: Macmillan Press, 1998: pp.163-188.

Hearst, David L., 'Twentieth-Century Pioneers', in *Tragicomedy*, London and New York: Methuen, 1984: pp.100-119.

Merchant, Moelwyn, 'The Status of Comedy', in *Comedy*, London and New York: Methuen, 1984: pp.1-6.

Murray, Patrick, 'The Dramatists: Journey into Silence', in *The Tragic Comedian: A Study of Samuel Beckett*, Cork: Mercier Press, 1970: pp.64-82.

3. Articles

Bouvier, Michel and Leutrat, Jean-Louis, 'Retour au Burlesque', in *Cahiers du Cinéma*, No.296, January 1997: pp.16-18.

Chion, Michel, 'Le dernier Mot du Muet', in *Cahiers du Cinéma*, No.330, December 1981: pp.4-15.